THE BEAST

THE BEAST

ADEBAYO AKINFENWA

MY STORY

with Damien McSorley

HEADLINE

First published in Great Britain in 2017
by HEADLINE PUBLISHING GROUP

1

Cataloguing in Publication Data is available from the British Library

Hardback ISBN 978 1 4722 4793 3

Typeset in Bliss Light by Palimpsest Book Production Limited, Falkirk, Stirlingshire

Printed and bound by
CPI Group (UK) Ltd, Croydon, CR0 4YY

Headline's policy is to use papers that are natural, renewable and recyclable products and made from wood grown in sustainable forests. The logging and manufacturing processes are expected to conform to the environmental regulations of the country of origin.

HEADLINE PUBLISHING GROUP
An Hachette UK Company
Carmelite House
50 Victoria Embankment
London EC4Y 0DZ

www.headline.co.uk
www.hachette.co.uk

I dedicate this book to my bloodline, my family. I admire sophistication, I admire self-belief, but I am firmly of the opinion that there is nothing better in this world than the mutual love and affection we hold for each other. I therefore thank Almighty God, Dad, Mum, Fausat, Yemi, Dele, Michelle, Kamira, Ajani, Jai, Kaliyah and Jaylan.

'From Hackney Marshes to the hallowed turf of Wembley. It doesn't get any better than that. Keep working hard. And for the ones who said I was too big to play football . . . HAHAHA!'

— *Adebayo Akinfenwa after scoring a penalty for AFC Wimbledon in the League Two play-off final (30 May 2016)*

CONTENTS

FOREWORD BY STEVEN GERRARD

Firstly, I would like to say it's a huge honour to write this foreword for Bayo. He is not only a star of League football in England but a top fella away from the game, too.

The first time I set eyes on Bayo I'm sure like a lot of people my first thoughts were, 'Wow he is a proper unit, an absolute man mountain'. I was glad we played in different leagues! Quite a few of my friends in football have competed against him for many years and they all agree he is a right handful to play against and a very dangerous striker in league football.

In January 2015 I got to sample that myself in the FA Cup. We met before kick-off and agreed to swap shirts after the game as he's a massive Liverpool fan. I found him to be a proper gentleman. During the game he gave our Liverpool backline all sorts of problems and even managed to score a well taken goal (well, it was a tap-in but don't tell him – ha). We managed to narrowly win 1-2 in the end, and at the end of the game I should have been coming away thinking about Liverpool FC and our progression to the next round of the FA cup but I couldn't stop thinking about how special it was for Bayo scoring against the team he's supported since he was a young boy. I knew a moment like that would live with him forever.

We've kept in touch and even had time to meet up in Los Angeles last year, spending a few hours talking football, our careers, future endeavours and family. He's always great company and I reckon he secretly holds the record for putting a giant burger away in the quickest time, or at least that's what I witnessed!

I look forward to watching him finish his football career in style and enjoying a successful career after playing. I have no doubt it'll be a massive success whatever he decides to do. My prediction is he'll be a big TV personality. His character and self-determination are something I greatly admire and this book really highlights that.

Good luck, big man.
Best wishes,
Stevie G

INTRODUCTION: REBEL WITH A CAUSE

Looks can be deceiving. That's not a secret. You might not think it to see me walking down the street, but I've always been charming. It's one of my strengths. I have one of those personalities that people gravitate towards. Anyone who knew me back in the day will tell you that. My mates, family, teachers. I think it's partly because of my size. Unless they already know me, people's first reaction when they meet me is often something approaching trepidation or even fear. I want people to respect me, and for the right reasons, not fear me, so the first thing I do is smile to put them at ease. It's always been a struggle to work against that misconception that people have of me just being a big, scary black guy. That's why I smile a lot, and try to be disarming and cool with people. I try to be warm and let people see beyond the image and the stereotype.

I know I'm not built like the average footballer. I'm 16 stone and in another life I might be a professional body builder. That's part of the reason so many people like me. I'm living proof that even in the modern game, which is overloaded with consummate athletes, you don't always have to fit into a neat little box. Do I think I'm a rebel? To an extent, yes I do. I never set out to be, but that's how it turned out. I'm late all the time, I never pay club fines, and I pretty much do my own thing. But my behaviour is never disrespectful or disruptive. It's not even like I'm ever deliberately late. I'm not trying to test anyone's patience. It is what it is. Shit happens!

All my life I've been bigger than most of the people around me. I never wanted that to be a factor, so I actively went out of my way to be a nice guy. I still do. There's no need to do otherwise. I didn't want to be seen as a bully. I hate bullies. But unfortunately, they are a part of life. People will get what they want by any means necessary. I was walking home from school one day with three other boys from the estate I lived on, when one of them called this younger kid over and said, 'What have you got for me?' The kid was panicking, and saying, 'What do you mean? I haven't got anything.' So the bigger kid asked him to jump up and down to make sure he didn't have anything in his pockets, then said he was going to take his hat or his bus pass. I really felt for the kid. His hat and bus pass were pretty much all he had. I know I should have stopped it right at the beginning. But at first, I just stood there. I couldn't believe what I was seeing. That kind of behaviour baffles me. How can someone treat another human being with such contempt and disrespect? The kid was so vulnerable, and there he was being violated. I couldn't stand by and watch, so I got his stuff back for him and told him to go about his business. The older kid didn't even argue with me, so you could say that in confrontational situations, my size has been a considerable advantage.

I'm not a pussy. I never will be. I do have a switch. Everyone does. I can look after myself. But unless you do me wrong, we're cool. That's always been my outlook on football, and life. I don't even mind when fans call me a fat bastard, or chant, 'I bet you're going for a doughnut,' when I make a run. It doesn't make it right. I'm at my place of work and you're abusing me. But I understand that it comes with the job. I love the relationship I have with the fans. It's been special and unique at every club I've been at. It's very humbling to have fans sing songs about you. Though obviously there are two sides to that coin. It's true that opposition fans only abuse the players they are afraid of. Nobody wastes their time booing bad players. They don't understand that, more often than not, hearing the abuse just makes us more determined to put one over on them. I usually get called fat, which is pretty boring. But I remember going on as sub at Portsmouth's Fratton Park and getting caught offside straight away. The next thing I know, the whole stadium, 15,000 people, are all singing, 'Akinfenwa! Your tits are offside!' I remember laughing so hard at that. Another time, when I was playing for Northampton Town, some of the opposition fans started singing, 'You're just a fat Eddie Murphy!' I was thinking . . . What? I don't even look like Eddie Murphy! It wasn't just plain abuse, they actually had jokes, and you have to respect that and take it on the chin. I don't even consider those kinds of incidents abusive. To me, it's more like banter. It doesn't get me down at all. Some people might look at it and say, 'Well, abuse is abuse.' They might have a point. But it's not racist, or offensive in any other way and I genuinely found it funny at the time. It's only when people get in my face off the pitch that I don't like it, because then I'm no longer at work. I'm still a footballer, but the game's over. Even though off the pitch I'm still representing my club, first and foremost I'm a man so don't disrespect me.

I was signing autographs after a game a while back when a kid came up and said to me, 'I bet you're going to eat all the pizzas on the bus.' That annoyed me a bit. I don't mind taking banter from the stands, but it makes it more personal when someone is right in front of you saying it to your face. I shut that shit down fast. I understand why they would say that stuff. I'm a big guy, and maybe the happy-go-lucky image I try so hard to portray makes people think they can say anything to me. But that was disrespectful, and I don't stand for it.

I often get judged before people meet me. They might see me walking down the street or see photos of me, and just make assumptions. It's part of human nature. Until five or six years ago when social media blew up, most of the people who saw me around thought I was a drug dealer. They would see a big black guy driving a nice car, put two and two together and get twenty. I have always played my football outside of the Premier League, so my games are rarely televised, and I'm not the type to go around telling everyone what I do for a living. They don't ask, so I don't tell them. I still get people I've known for years saying to me, 'I didn't know you played football!' Probably the only reason they know who I am now is because they saw me on *Soccer AM* or their kids play *FIFA* too much!

It's only the past couple of years where my profile has risen to the point where I'm getting stopped in the street. I always had two Twitter accounts, one for football-related stuff, and a personal one. I used to go clubbing a lot, and the people who know me outside the game always followed my personal one, not even having the slightest idea that the footballing account existed. I liked the fact that people didn't know what I did for a living. But then it got to the stage where there was no hiding place. Wherever I go now, it seems that everybody knows who I am. And for a League Two player that's no mean feat. I have no choice but to embrace it, and make it work for me. Social media is now a huge part of who I am.

People think it's easy to build and maintain this kind of profile on social media. They think all you have to do is play with your phone a bit and send out a couple of tweets or updates a week. But trust me, it's not that simple. It's very time-consuming for a start. It's work. I have a schedule, and I have to stick to it. People want to know my life. Obviously, if you're just looking to have fun with it, you can do it sporadically. There's no pressure. But if it's part of who you are, you have to invest the time. Like most things, the more you put into it the more you get out.

As much as I love the game, I always see footballers as hired help. We go to a club, and we do a job for as long as we're needed there. It is what it is. Supply and demand, like any other industry. I came to terms with that a long time ago. What's more, it's a game of many variables, top of the list being form, and that comes and goes. It's not an exact science, and there's rarely any kind of rhyme or reason to it. When you're on song, you're on song. And when you're not, you're not. It's that simple. What I don't like is other people like managers and coaches trying to take credit for things I do. They might say things like, 'Oh, I stuck with him through all those bad times, and helped make him the player he is.' Obviously there are tons of people on the periphery that help your career along. But ultimately you have to do it alone. When you're out there playing, you can't hide. The football pitch can be a lonely place.

Don't get me wrong, playing football is a good job, but it's a scary job. If you get injured, or if you have a dip in form, it can take a good deal of time to get your mojo back and in some cases players never do. Everything can change in a second. Away from the glamour and riches of Europe's elite, if you find yourself without a club you have to go searching, and you'll be one of a thousand players doing just that at any one time. It's more real in the lower leagues, because all you need is a season or two in the Premier League, or the top end of the Championship, and you should be pretty much set for life. You can certainly afford to spend six months or so out of the game waiting for the right opportunity to come along. Most footballers miss out on a proper education because they're too busy playing football. That's the reality of it. As one of a thousand lower division footballers without a club, you only have a limited time until you become one of a million unemployed and unqualified workers on the scrapheap. I don't think many people outside the game realise that. Footballers aren't robots. We all have dips in form, and what works for one player might not work for another. We are all just finding our way, and trying to do right by ourselves and our families.

I never went through a football academy, so I was never institutionalised by it. Another way of looking at it would be to say I was never programmed by anybody. I'm my own man. I'm an imposing figure, and I'm never afraid to say what I think. I've learned something at every club I've been at. I've always tried to enjoy my life, and take that attitude onto the football field. I do realise how lucky I am to have the career I've had. I've been a professional footballer for eighteen years. Some players have one season, then they are finished. Lots of players don't even have that. Sometimes I still experience things where I have to check myself to make sure it's real. I did Hoops Aid, the charity basketball match at Wembley, and David James was my captain. So I was chatting to him, which for me being a Liverpool supporter was amazing enough, but then the actor Colin Salmon came up and asked me for a photo. I was like, 'What? *You* want *my* photo?' At one point, the security had to stop me signing autographs because it turned into a stampede. The whole thing was mind-boggling. The cult of celebrity is something I'm cool with, but not something I'll ever get used to. I've never had media training at any of my clubs, and I never get told what I can say or what I can't say. I just go in there with an open mind and be me. It's much better that way. More natural. Because there's nothing scripted and what you see is what you get.

Recently I did something for Sky with Paul Merson and Matt Le Tissier, and before that I did something with George North, the Welsh rugby international, for Gillette. Not so long ago I did an appearance with Jimmy Floyd Hasselbaink and people were giving me more attention than him. That, to me, was all kinds of wrong. I've achieved things in the game, but this guy is an out-and-out legend. He played for Chelsea, Atlético Madrid, Holland. I grew up watching him. I felt like saying to everyone, 'Don't you know who this man is? What's wrong with you? Give him some props!'

Another misconception people have of me is that because my profile is so high, and my social media following so big, I must have Premiership money. I don't. Far from it. Not all footballers are on £2 million-plus a year. In fact, the average annual salary for a player in League Two where I play is more like £40,000. That isn't much more than the average working man earns and his career will be twice as long as a footballer's. It's only the past ten years or so that the Premier League has gone crazy with money. Maybe in time some of that money will trickle down to the lower leagues, but it hasn't happened yet.

Despite being a professional footballer most of my adult life, and now being a media personality with my own clothing company, I've never been rich. I'm from a working-class background, and that's still very much the case. But because I'm only a League Two footballer, it doesn't mean I don't have anything to say. People can relate to me because I'm *not* rich, the same way they relate to Conor McGregor. Four or five years ago he was on the dole, then he fought Floyd Mayweather in one of the biggest money fights in history. Everyone loves fairy-tale stories about people from modest backgrounds making good because it gives them hope. It shows them that they are in control of their own destiny, and those dreams they have really do come true if they are prepared to put the work in.

I don't go out of my way to make people like me. I don't want people to dislike me, either. All I can do is be myself, be authentic, don't bullshit anyone, and let them make their own minds up. All I want is for people who meet me to walk away knowing that what I show them isn't a front, or a facade, it's the real me. No matter what happens in life, I'll always be a down-to-earth brother.

Despite never reaching the Premier League, I've been lucky. It's a given that I've been lucky away from football with my beautiful family and the life I have, but even in football I've been lucky. The fans have loved me at every club I've played for, and I've scored goals at them all. I've been a figurehead and a cult hero to thousands of people all over the country. I'm a target man. I put my body on the line, and every week I go into battle for the club I'm playing for. The fans know what they're going to get with me, and I think they respond to and appreciate that.

1 LIFE IN THE CAGE

I was born on 10 May 1982, and spent my early years on Mayville council estate in Islington, north London. We lived on the top floor of a block. My dad was Muslim and my mum was Christian. They were very strict. Especially my mum. The whole estate knew that. If anyone heard my mum calling me it was like, 'B, you better get upstairs. Now.' Both my parents were out most of the time working, so my older sister Fausat bossed the house and looked after me and my two brothers, Yemi, who is older than me and Dele, who is younger. She made sure we had dinner and did our homework, and she had to grow up fast to take on that responsibility. My sister was born in Nigeria, and came over when she was about five. In the meantime, my older brother who was born in Belgium was convinced for the first three years of his life that he was an only child because he'd never met our sister.

Because she spent so long there, the Nigerian influence was much stronger in my sister than in us. Now we all fully embrace it. She was very traditional. She loved sport, especially athletics. She was a sprinter. In that sense, she was an early role-model. As a female specimen she was solid, and she could fight! When the estate bully pushed over one of my brothers, she went and sorted him out. And his mate. The first person ever to punch me in my face was my own sister. I must have been about thirteen, and she was six years older. There were some peanuts on the living room table, and I wanted some. But my mum had a house guest, and she told me I couldn't. So I walked out of the room, swearing under my breath just as I passed my sister. She goes, 'What did you say?' and before I could answer she punched me in the face! As if that wasn't enough, my mum came out to see what was going on, my sister grassed me up, and then I got a slap off my mum, too! Even now we're both adults, my sister still doesn't like it if I swear in front of her.

I always had a reputation for being the rebel of the house. But it was never a conscious decision, and I was never a rebel in the classic sense of the word. I wasn't a trouble-maker. It was my own stubbornness that got me in trouble more than anything. If I wanted to do something, I wouldn't let anything dissuade me. It was like I would get fixated on it. Sometimes that single-mindedness can be a blessing, but other times it can be a curse. It was a close-knit, loving family, and quite religious. I don't know if it's an African trait, but we siblings have a hierarchy, primarily based on age. The older you are in comparison to others, the more respect you get. We clash sometimes, but there is definitely a hierarchy in place, with our big sister, or surrogate parent, at the top of it. It manifests itself in some strange ways. The youngest person there will always get the last piece of chicken, and the oldest person in the group will always sit in the front passenger seat of the car. It's just the dynamic we have, and we all have to find our place within the system.

I never thought of us as being poor, because we never went hungry and we always had the essentials. Our upbringing was a long way from lavish, but we were always fed and clothed. We didn't have the flash Nike trainers and stuff, but that's more because those things weren't as accessible then as they are now. If there was something we wanted, we'd have to tell our parents in January and then we'd have it for Christmas after they'd saved for it the rest of the year. That was just the way it was. One year, one of my brothers asked for an Amstrad games console and told our mum and dad he needed it for school. We all knew he just wanted to play *Football Manager* on it!

I remember finding it really hard to get an ice cream from the ice cream van when I was a kid. It would come around the estate and all the other kids would rush out and fill their boots, but I never had the money to do that. My parents' logic was, 'Why spend £1 on a cone from the van when you can spend the same amount of money and get ten choc-ices from the supermarket?' I was always a bit jealous of those people who could just roll up and drop £1 whenever they wanted without even thinking about it. It did me a lot of good, though. I still carry a bit of that philosophy with me now. I'm sensible with money. I'm not wasteful or extravagant. There's no need to be. You can still get what you want and not be flash about it.

Despite the lack of ice cream, my parents were very fixated on doing right by us. They made sure my brothers and sister went to university, and were wise enough to realise that even as a kid I lived and breathed football. I knew I was going to turn professional some day, or at least make a living in the sport somehow, and told them so. I was very determined from a young age. There must have come a point when either my mum or my dad said, 'Look, all B cares about is playing football. He's never going to university. He's never going to work in a bank or anything. So we may as well support him as much as we can.'

I didn't even care what I dressed like. It was never on my radar. Sometimes, other kids on the estate would make comments. Never to my face, but when I wasn't around. It was water off a duck's back. I just wanted to play football. I thought about it day and night. I'd even have dreams about it. I used to go to school wearing church shoes, with the pointy toes. I look back and laugh now, but I'd have been very happy wearing football kit every day to school.

My parents have been the biggest single influence on me. They still are. I'm your classic mummy's boy. Mum has been the star shining the brightest all my life. I know it's a cliché, but I really feel blessed to have her. Even now, if she calls me and tells me to go to the house, I'll drop whatever I'm doing and get over there. Pronto. You don't want to keep my mum waiting! When I was growing up, she was very big on respecting your elders, and doing the right thing. If I ever told someone on the estate to shut up or something and it got back to her, she would go absolutely berserk. People often ask me how I never got caught up in the gangster life, or went to jail. Well, she's probably the main reason. I was never scared of the police, or the other kids on the estate who were into all kinds of sketchy shit. I was scared of my mum!

My mum was pretty rough with me. The thing I appreciated most was after I'd got a hiding, my mum would wait an hour or so, then call me into the room and explain why she'd done it. As a kid, you need that. It puts things into context and helps you better understand why whatever you did was wrong. For some reason, it also made me not hold grudges. There's a flash-point, and then you have to put it behind you.

Mum wasn't just a positive influence on me. All the family would say that the reason we worked so well as a unit was because of her. She's very traditional in many ways. Old-school Nigerian. But she's been in England most of her life, so over time she's kind of tweaked her habits and mannerisms to fit in more with Western culture. In my household there was very little in the way of sharing opinions. It was more a case of, 'Yo. You need to do this.' Now, because she's been here longer, there's more debate and conversation. Only now can I have some idea of how difficult things were for her back then. She was very intense, but you get a different take on life as you get older and become parents yourselves. Now, looking back, I can see why she did things a certain way, though it wasn't always obvious at the time. Me and my brothers and sister can now see things from the outside and laugh about it. Especially as most of us have kids of our own. That said, I have no idea how my dad puts up with it. It's easy for me – when it gets too much I can just leave the house, but that poor man is stuck there!

My dad is a Tottenham fan, for some reason. There was a running joke in the family that I was his favourite, just because he liked football. My Pops was the first male figure in my life who showed me the true meaning of hard work. He had two jobs and later in life he educated me on being a father myself. We were lucky to have a true role model. Mum was the glue that held the family together, the decision maker, and he would be like the enforcer going around making sure everything was done the way she wanted. All my brothers and sisters were confident in whatever they did, but I think there's a special kind of confidence that comes from being a third child, or a middle child. You're not the older, more responsible one, and you're not the spoiled baby of the family, so you have to stand up for yourself and make your voice heard. I think that's why I've always been opinionated, and never been afraid to speak up.

Back in the day, everyone used to hang out at the bottom of the stairs in my block. It was predominantly a boys' estate. Any outsider who met us probably thought we were some kind of crew or gang, but the truth was it was just boys living there. We were all about the same age and played football together, so of course we all hung out. If there were any girls living there, we never noticed them. As soon as you came out of the estate, there was a football cage. From there you could see all the cars coming in. When I was five or six, my friends and I developed a bird call. Like an early warning system. Everyone knew how strict my parents were, so as soon as anyone saw their car turn in, my friends would give this call which would be my signal to dart across the estate and get back to my flat before my parents got there. I had some pretty close shaves. Looking back, they probably guessed a few times that I was out playing football.

I would be in that cage after school every night. During the school holidays, as soon as my parents left for work I would meet the boys and we'd spend eight or ten hours a day in there just balling. There would be so many of us, we'd have to play what we called 'four benches'. We had one touch and four goals, and the object was to get people out. Let me tell you, the competition was intense! There was just a constant progression of boys wanting to play. Otherwise, we might play 'sixty seconds'. If you don't know what that is, you're missing out! There'd only be one goalie, and you had sixty seconds to score a goal past him. The catch was, it had to be on the volley, and the last person to touch it before the time was up then had to go and have a turn in goal. It was how we got around the fact that nobody ever wanted to play in goal. That was football at its most pure, before the politics and drama kicked in. We were just playing for the sheer enjoyment it brought us.

There was another game we used to play called 'halfway', which was basically about not letting the ball pass the halfway line. You weren't allowed in the area, and there were no goalies. There were just two people on the pitch at any one time, so pretty much the only way you could score was by chipping the ball over the other player. He could use his hands, catch it like a goalkeeper, whatever, but you had to get the ball over him. It was good practice for taking free-kicks, where you have to get the ball up, over the wall, and down into the net. My brother Yemi was a far better player than me at that stage. He was three years older than me, and the complete footballer – big, strong, quick, skilful. He was *that guy*. To get the ball over him I would have to spin it, wait for it to come down, then side-foot it over his head. We were training ourselves to a really high standard, and not even realising it at the time. To us, we were just playing games. We were always active. If we didn't have a football, we'd race cars on foot.

The first time I ever had that feeling about football where you think, 'You know what? I can do this!' was when I was about five. I used to watch Yemi play with his mates. Three years is a big gap at that age. There was obviously a big size difference, as well as a difference in skill levels. Yemi was a proper baller.

I was still toe-punting the ball all the time, the way you do when you first start learning to play, but he would be doing side-foots and all these different skills. I used to try to copy him. All I wanted to do was play with him and his mates, and I remember one day they let me join in. That acknowledgement from the older estate boys meant a lot at the time. They didn't let just anyone play with them. It was a massive compliment and gave my confidence a huge boost.

Newington Green Primary School had a youth club, or an after-school play centre, and I used to go there to play. One of the guys who coached us was called Steve Spooner. He was about six foot two which made him an absolute giant when we were kids. He commanded respect because you literally had no choice but to look up to him. I remember him telling me when I was six or seven how much better I was at football than the other boys in my age group. To be fair, I was much bigger than them, but the main thing was all I cared about was football. I never had any aspirations of ever doing anything else, so I invested all my energy into it. Every spare moment I had, I'd be kicking a ball around. If I didn't have anyone else to play with, I'd happily play by myself. I would test myself all the time. A hundred kick-ups, fifty headers; my skill level was improving daily. I sometimes get people telling me I haven't achieved as much as a footballer as I could have, such was the amount of potential I had. There was nothing I couldn't do with a football at my feet. People who knew me back then say, 'Man, I thought you'd be playing in the Premier League.' Until a few years ago, that used to hurt my feelings. It almost made me feel like a failure, or at least like I hadn't done as well in the game as I could have. But when I think about it, I've done all right for a lad from a council estate. I have a good living doing what I love, and I've played consistently at a high level for most of my career and had some fantastic experiences.

As a kid, if someone had a reputation on the football field, if they were talked about, I couldn't wait to take them on to see how I matched up. It brought the best out of me. We played one of the local schools, and I'm sure I played against Paolo Vernazza (later of Watford, Arsenal and Rotherham United). He was their top boy, and I was our top boy. I remember the pitch being so big! Paolo was gifted. I mean, technically gifted. When I look back at my own game, there really wasn't much I couldn't do, but he was head and shoulders above me and everyone else. He just did everything better. When he had the ball, he seemed to glide across the pitch effortlessly. He might not even remember this, but one time he knocked the ball past me so I gave him a little dig, and he went flying into these plant pots we kept at the side of the pitch. He might have been faster and more skilful than me, but he wasn't stronger.

The classroom at our primary school was split right down the middle. I was an avid Liverpool fan because back then, in the late eighties, it was a golden period and Liverpool were winning everything. I was a massive John Barnes fan. As far as footballing heroes goes, he was it. But a lot of lads followed Arsenal because they were the local team. Arsenal used to send coaches around some of the schools. They were decent coaches, but they would always focus on the basics, like trapping the ball or laying it off. I was the best player in my age group by far, and had surpassed that standard long ago. So when the Arsenal coaches would come around and try teaching me how to pass a ball, I'd be like, 'How about you teach me something I don't know?'

One day, this Arsenal coach had me doing drills with one of my classmates. I was quick as a kid, so I would burn down the line, flick the ball inside, and my classmate would score. We did the same move dozens of times. The coach said, 'I like you two, how about you come down to train at the club?' The Liverpool supporters in my class were like, 'You can't do that!' I actually remember saying to the Arsenal scout, 'Nah, sorry mate. I can't. I support Liverpool.'

The first time I remember feeling the thrill of scoring a goal was when I was about nine. I played in a schools final for Newington Green at Highbury Fields, and half the school came to watch us. It was 0-0, and I was facing off against this defender. I'd drop my shoulder to go one way, and he'd do the exact same thing. This went on for about twenty seconds. It was hilarious. I could hear our coach Steve Spooner calling from the sideline, 'Just knock it past him and go!' He always drilled into us that there's more than one way to beat a defender. If you can't beat him with skill, find another way. In the second half, I was outside the area when the ball came out to me. I just smashed it, and caught it perfectly. The ball flew through the air, off the bar and into the goal. All the kids watching on the sidelines went mental. Paul Merson had just scored a blinding goal for Arsenal, and we'd all seen it on the telly. He did this mad 'rocket' celebration. So when the goal went in, I ran off and did the Merson celebration. From that moment I was like, 'This is it. This is what I want to do.' It was like a drug. I needed to experience that feeling again.

One Tuesday night not long after, the youth club had a kids disco. There were cupcakes and music. It was a great laugh. I was playing for a local side then, and we had training. But training was cancelled. So obviously, I went to the disco instead. But then, about an hour before training started, someone rang my house phone and said training was back on. My sister came down to the disco to tell me, and the moment I heard I put down the cupcake I was holding, sprinted home, and got changed into my tracksuit ready for training. That was one of the watershed moments when the people around me started to think, 'This kid really loves football. He even loves it more than discos and cupcakes.'

When I left Newington Green Primary, I went to Highbury Grove comprehensive secondary school in Islington. At the time, Highbury Grove was known as a fighting school. It was a pretty rough inner city establishment. There were a few in the same area; Holloway was another one. Both boys' schools. If you went to Highbury Grove, you had to be able to handle yourself. My brother Yemi going there first helped me a lot, because he already had a reputation. By the time I started there, he was in his final year. He wasn't one for arguing, he would just sort people out. He was one of the top three fighters in the school. As a first year, if anyone gave me any shit, I'd just go running to him. I remember playing money up the wall once, losing, and then when the other lad asked me for his winnings I mugged him off and went to find my big brother!

Another time I was running up a staircase and this boy called Longhead banged me in the chest for no reason. This kid was bigger and older than me. He was in my brother's year. I always thought, 'If you don't have a reason to do something, why do it?' This Longhead character, not knowing who I was, and more importantly, who my brother was, just banged me in the chest for nothing. So that lunchtime, I went and told Yemi. He didn't even let me finish my sentence, he just said, 'Show me the boy.' When we found Longhead, I was in awe at the effect my brother had on him. He didn't have to hit him or kick off in any way. As soon as Longhead realised whose little brother he'd been messing with, he went to pieces. I'd never seen someone apologise so profusely. After that, if anyone gave me any trouble, someone would whisper in their ear, 'Don't you know whose brother that is?'

Yemi was never a gangster. He was just a guy who could handle himself, and wasn't afraid to prove it. For that reason alone, people gave him respect. I looked up to him, and I remember thinking that was exactly how I wanted to be when I grew up. I didn't want to be one of the boys who were feared because they might stick a knife in you. I just wanted to be respected for the person I was and the things I did. Luckily for me, thanks to my brother, I never had to have a single fight. I rode his name all through school, and even after he left. But I quickly got out of the habit of using him to solve all my problems, because you don't earn respect like that. I started going about doing things my own way.

• • •

When I was about eleven or twelve, I asked my mum if I could go out one Sunday. She said no, so I snuck out anyway and ended up going to this park with my mate Victor. There was a guy playing football there with a couple of kids, so we asked if we could join in. Victor wasn't exceptional at football, but he was steady. This game was easy for me, I was ghosting through everyone. After seeing me play, the guy, whose name was Steve, asked me if I played for anybody. I said no. So he asked me if I would like to. I said, 'Yeah, why not?' He said okay, but he was going to have to speak to my parents about it first. And that's what he did. He was really polite and approachable, and put any concerns my parents might have had to rest. He even offered to pick me up every Sunday and take me over to Wanstead to play. I cheekily asked if he would sign my mate Victor, too. He asked Vic what position he played and I whispered, 'Say midfield!' Despite my best efforts, I don't think Vic ever even showed up for training. He just wasn't into it as much as I was. For him, football wasn't the be-all and end-all like it was for me.

It turned out this Steve was the manager of Senrab FC's Under-12s side. Senrab FC, which takes its name from Senrab Street in Stepney, is one of the most famous Sunday League teams in the country. It's most widely known for its Chelsea links. In fact, some people call it Chelsea Juniors. The two clubs aren't officially affiliated, but they may as well be because John Terry, Ray Wilkins, Gary Chivers, Ray Lewington and Tommy Langley all went on to play for Chelsea after starting out at Senrab. In addition, the likes of Ugo Ehiogu (Aston Villa, Middlesbrough and England), Sol Campbell (Tottenham Hotspur, Arsenal and England) David Kerslake (Spurs, Swindon, QPR), Ledley King (Tottenham Hotspur and England), Paul Konchesky (Charlton Athletic, Leicester City and England), Ade Akinbiyi (Norwich City, Gillingham, Stoke City and Nigeria), Jlloyd Samuel (Aston Villa, Bolton Wanderers and Trinidad & Tobago) and Bobby Zamora (Brighton & Hove Albion, West Ham United and England) also came from there. The list is endless.

I can't remember exactly how it happened, probably because of my size and build, but when I started at Senrab I played at centre-back rather than up front. My parents were very supportive about anything football-related, even when the time came to stump up £25 or £30 for boots to play in. It was a lot for them. They gave me the money, and I went out and bought a pair of black and purple Hi-Tecs for about £20, if not less. I could have got myself a more expensive pair. But because we didn't have much money, whenever I was entrusted with some I was in the habit of always taking the cheaper option and pocketing the change. That was my first ever pair of football boots.

Yemi was also playing a lot of football at the time, and he

also needed boots. But my parents couldn't afford two pairs so our manager had to buy his. He actually got the better deal, because he got a sick pair of black and blue Puma Kings. He played a game against Gifton Noel-Williams (Watford, Stoke City, Burnley) and actually got the better of him. He said it was because of the new boots. I still think my brother could have had a big future in the game. In my mind's eye I see him on a par with Ledley King. They were similar kinds of player. But Yemi gave football up because he wanted to be a singer instead, the doughnut. Still, when he gave up football he gave me his Puma Kings, so it all worked out for the best and I ended up with the good pair of boots after all.

One day, I went in to training and told Steve I was sick of playing in defence and wanted a go as a striker. He looked at me as if to say, 'Since when have you been a striker?', but to his credit he relented and gave me a chance up front. We won 7-1 and I scored six goals. From that game on, I was a striker. Except one time, when we entered a tournament with a team connected to Islington & District. It was kind of the best of the best, comprising all these boys picked from various teams. I played centre-back for them just because the manager didn't know me very well, and he thought he had better options up front than me. I can't say he was wrong because we won 4-1 at Fulham's Craven Cottage in the final.

Being a defender was my back-up option. Let's be honest, I looked like a defender and I could intimidate and out-muscle most other players when I needed to. Because I wanted to play so much, if I couldn't get into a team any other way, I'd happily play at the back. I do think that helped me as the years went on and my career progressed. Playing in that position helps you get into the mind of the centre-back and puts you in a position to beat him easier when you're playing as a forward.

Senrab opened my eyes to a lot. I was the year below John Terry and Jlloyd Samuel. Their team used to go out and win every game 12–1. It was ridiculous. Jlloyd Samuel used to score six or seven goals a game. He was a machine. That's why it was so funny seeing him at Villa years later playing at right-back. He was never a right-back when I knew him! Their manager, a guy called Paul, was big mates with our manager, Steve, and they were the ones who introduced me to pub life. We used to go out in Wanstead after training or after a match for a game of pool, and they would drop me off at home afterwards. Steve was a taxi driver, which was convenient.

I loved nothing better than playing tournaments with Senrab. You'd rock up at midday on a Sunday, then depending how far you went, you might be there until seven or eight at night, just kicking a ball around. We didn't get much in the way of support. We never needed it. I can't speak for the other players, but my parents were always working and couldn't afford to take days off, my younger brother was my younger brother, so he was just annoying, and my older brother and sister were just doing their own thing. Throughout my career, I've never expected everyone I know to come and watch me play. Obviously it's nice, especially if it's a big game, but I've always gone out and done it by myself. I've always understood that other people have other responsibilities. The whole world doesn't revolve around me playing football. It goes back to when my parents were always working when I was growing up. It's not that they weren't supportive, they were just work-oriented.

At school, I found the football pitch to be a great leveller. There, it didn't matter if the team I was playing against were older or bigger than me, I always felt I had an advantage. Part of that was ego-driven, because I knew that if things ever escalated my brother had my back. But at the same time the football field was where I was best able to express myself. I never truly believed I was that much better than everyone else, but that was how it felt and I fed off that confidence. The teachers all knew I wasn't academically inclined. I was too into my football. I wouldn't say they were supportive, but they let me get on with it. I think I was just a nonentity to most of them. I was never going to pass loads of exams, but at the same time I wasn't getting into trouble all the time, either. I suppose they all just had other things to worry about.

Some of the teachers thought I was a bully because a lot of the younger kids who I played football with would come up and give me sweets, just because I let them play with me. I would always let the younger kids play. Because I was so much better than the other kids, it wouldn't devalue the team at all. There was one teacher called Mr Pants, funnily enough, who was especially suspicious of me – but luckily the younger kids would tell him, 'Nah. Bayo's my friend!'

Now, looking back, maybe there was an element of psychological manipulation on my part. I knew what I had to do to get sweets. But like I said, despite my size, I've never gone out of my way to make teammates or even the people I played against afraid of me. I never wanted that. I've always tried to be cool with everyone I meet.

Me and both my brothers are all big. I don't think there's anything hereditary in the Akinfenwa family. My mum and dad are both small. Their dads were said to be big, but I never got to see any of my grandparents, they all passed before I was born, so I can't say for sure. All I've ever really known is the six of us: Mum and Dad, and the four siblings. My younger brother had to work on being big. He started lifting weights when he was still in school. But me and my older brother are just naturally big. I never did weights until much later when I signed for Swansea City. When I went there, nobody believed that I didn't do weights so I thought I might as well do them anyway.

My school reports always said I was charming and I smiled a lot. I wasn't the type to be up to mischief, being a menace and getting detentions. One thing I learned about teachers is that they've heard it all before. There's nothing you could say or do that would ever be new to them. On parents' evenings, they would say to my mum and dad, 'As you probably know, B wants to be a footballer. But everyone wants to be a footballer. So make sure he has a back-up plan if it doesn't work out for him.'

They were right, too. It's something I tell my own kids now. As determined as I was to succeed, you just don't know what's around the corner, and it pays off to be as prepared as you can possibly be. That's why I stayed in school. My being an outstanding footballer was all well and good, but I had enough smarts about me to know that there were plenty of other outstanding footballers out there who, for one reason or another, had never made it big.

My house, as they called it back then at my school, Highbury Grove, was called Marlborough and our colour was purple. Then there were Richmond, Gloucester and York. Every year we would have a sports competition which included football. My class had two or three ballers, but Richmond probably had the best overall team. They were also street boys, so not only could they play but they could intimidate you, too. Despite never having a fight at school, I was known as one of the top three fighters. (That was mainly my brother's doing. He fought so I didn't have to.) We all knew that it was better that the three of us never actually fought each other, just so nobody would ever really know who was the hardest. We made sure we never crossed paths. It was all about 'what-ifs and maybes'. Sometimes, that seed of uncertainty in someone's mind is enough.

There are times in a man's life, though, where he has to stand up for himself. One evening when I was thirteen or fourteen, my dad sent my younger brother to come and get me. But I was hanging with my mates at the youth centre after school, and didn't want to go home. So I just said, 'Yeah, whatever.' Time went on, and I completely forgot I was supposed to be going home. Then suddenly, the boys I was with all just went silent. I'm thinking, 'What's wrong?' I turned around and my dad was standing there with a face like thunder. He just had to say my name in this special tone that he has, to make my knees start shaking. When I heard him say it like that, I knew I was in trouble. He still does it now. He didn't show his anger. He just said, 'Get upstairs.'

On the way home, I did that thing that kids do when they know they're going to get a slap when they walk really slowly. You keep your eyes open, and wait for the hand. Then, when you see it coming, you speed up a bit to take some of the force out of it. It's all about the timing. Anyway, it didn't work, and I copped a good one on the back of the head. This isn't one of those 'poor me' stories where I complain about my folks giving me a hard time. I'm just trying to illustrate how strict they were, and I probably needed that discipline at various points in my life, especially growing up. If I'd listened to my brother and gone home when I was supposed to, I wouldn't have got a slap.

The next day, it got back to me that one of the kids on the estate heard about me getting smacked and was laughing about it. Taking the piss out of me. The kid who said it was cousins with the boy who kind of ran the estate, so for about two days there was this 'will they, won't they' tension around us. For me, it was a pretty big deal. I had to repair my shattered reputation. When I finally confronted the kid, at first he tried to act tough. But in the end he backed down and I was like, 'Cool! Got my rep back and didn't even have to fight!'

Despite me being in it, out of all the years at Highbury Grove, mine probably had the worst football team of all. In fact, my year wasn't great at anything. Not fighting, football, athletics. It was a bit of a miss-year for some reason. There were four schools in the same area who were all known for their footballing ability: Highbury Grove, Holloway, Central Foundation and St Aloysius. I was at Highbury Grove, Jay Bothroyd (Wolves, Cardiff City, QPR and England) was at Holloway, Joe Cole (West Ham United, Chelsea, Liverpool and England) was at St Aloysius, and there was a guy called Benno at Central Foundation. We were the top boys. The best players. In my final year, we played Joe Cole's St Aloysius in a semi-final. They were a good team. But we had a midfielder called Samuel who completely marked Joe Cole out of the game and we ended up winning 3-2. That was one of the best games I've ever played in, because it was such an accomplishment to beat them. Nobody had given us a chance.

We met Holloway in the final. It was such a big deal, almost my entire family came to that game only to see us lose 8-2. I got the two goals though, and the second one was a ridiculous bicycle kick. It was made all the sweeter because during the game some of my brother's friends who'd come to watch were trying to convince him that I wasn't a striker. After the bicycle kick went in, they started going, 'Yeah, maybe B's a striker after all.'

Either because of my skill level or my size, as a youngster I tended to dominate the teams I played on. I always felt a sense of responsibility, so I always made sure I kept my temperament in check. I was usually the 'go-to' guy, and I knew that without me the team probably wouldn't have a chance of winning the game. Also, no matter how passionate I was, I never stopped enjoying football. It was always still a game, and always fun to me. I remember when my estate started a football team, and none of my so-called mates would tell me about it because they knew that if I showed up, I'd dominate things and make it all about me. I caught them all going to training one evening and followed them. When I got there, I met the coach, a guy called Paul, and asked him if I could play. At first he said no, because they'd already picked the teams. After a bit of pleading, he said, 'Okay, if you can do thirty kick-ups, you're in.'

Obviously, I rattled off thirty kick-ups like it was nothing, and training started. He was showing us how to mark, and he had me helping him. He put me in a position and said to the other boys, 'Look, B's got nowhere to go.' So with that, I dropped a shoulder, scooped the ball up, flicked it over his head, and brought it back down again on the line. I used to do things like that all the time, so to me it was no big deal, and the boys watching all knew what I could do so it was nothing new to them, either. But Paul had never met me before, and when he saw me do that, he was in awe.

The upshot of all this was that the estate formed an eight-a-side team, which would play every Friday night over at Market Road. It was only estate boys, but we had a solid team with a good spine. One lad who played for us, Arhan, he was like Xavi. He was a small kid, but strong and skilful with a great range of passing. The one advantage I felt we had over other teams was that most of them were from nicer areas. We had that hard, streetwise edge to us, so we could intimidate when we needed to. We played St Mary's Youth Club, who had a really good reputation, over two legs, and I remember we must have terrified them in the first leg because for the second they brought Shaun Wright-Phillips (Manchester City, Chelsea, QPR) to play us. The minute we saw him, everyone was like, 'Oh shit. That's Ian Wright's son.' You could tell he was a class apart. He would pick the ball up, take it the length of the pitch, and bang it in the top corner of the net without anyone getting near him, let alone tackling him. It was frightening. They ended up beating us 2-1, but only because they had Shaun playing for them.

The sad thing was the estate team only had funding for a year, then it folded. There's no telling how far we could have gone had we been allowed to.

2 TOEING THE LINE

Steve, my manager at Senrab, had his connections, like most coaches and managers do at that level. Through him, scouts from clubs like Charlton Athletic and Leyton Orient would come down and watch us play on Sundays. It was around this time that I developed Osgood–Schlatter Disease (OSD) in my knees. OSD is quite common among youngsters who play a lot of sport. One of the main causes is overuse. It's basically an inflammation of the cartilage or tendon at the top of the tibia (shin bone). Steve at Senrab was friendly with one of the physios at Charlton, so he drove me down there and got me diagnosed. It isn't that serious, and usually resolves itself given time. But it's very painful and it did hold me back a little. It even put me out of the game completely for a while.

Looking back, like most kids, I was probably playing and training too much. It's a criticism often levelled at British football. It's not unusual to have kids playing in four or five different teams at the same time. That means they can be playing competitive matches almost every day of the week, plus training. The better you are, the more people want you to play for them. Also, it doesn't help that in the UK kids often play on full-size pitches, whereas on the continent they play on smaller ones. With less space to work the ball in, there is more emphasis placed on improving your skill. Here, it's more about stamina and positioning. It can be the hardest thing to reel yourself in, and you need someone there looking out for you to tell you when you're overdoing it. With Senrab, most of the time we would train over in Canary Wharf and Steve, who only lived about fifteen minutes away, would pick me up and drop me off. He kind of took me under his wing and became that person.

I was lucky in that I usually escaped the violence and most of the shit other boys my age seemed to be going through. I mostly hang with my brothers, and apart from them I have a small but close group of friends. Guys I grew up with. Everybody needs that. Your old friends keep you grounded. I always wanted people to say that I was authentic, and I never changed. One of my mates, Victor, I've known since I was three. We went through both primary and comprehensive school together. My best mate is a guy called Regal, who I've known since I was eleven. We met at Highbury Grove. Regal is his nickname, he's a rapper. His real name is Alroy. As kids, whenever we met people we would change our names just for the fun of it. I was known as Prince, and he was Jamal. They are my boys. Then, there are my younger brother's people, Del and Kenneth, who I've known all their lives. We're so close, I classify them as family. I'm very selective who I let into my inner circle. In fact, there's only been one relatively recent one, and that's Mike, who's been a mate for the last eight years or so. When I was growing up, there was never a sense of people being with me, or attaching themselves to me, because of what I might be able to do for them. Luckily, I never had those relationships. It was just a case of all being boys on the estate, and all being into football. But I would say that among those who did hang out with me, there was never any doubt that I would be a footballer.

I say I usually escaped all the violence and most of the shit other boys my age seemed to be going through, but there was one incident that stands out. I was in my last year at Highbury Grove, so it would have been 1997 or '98. This was around the time there were a lot of Triads coming into London. During lunchtimes, me and my friends often went up to Highbury Fields because being from a boys' school, that was the only place we could chat to girls. It was where we all mixed together. One day we went there, and there was a group of Chinese lads. Something happened, words were exchanged, and the upshot was these four Chinese lads beat up a young kid. They beat up one or two others as well. Then the rumours started going around that the school was under siege by Triads. They definitely won the early exchanges. But you know, whatever you do in life, there are always comebacks and consequences.

One day, we found out they were all waiting down the road after school, so we rounded up all our top boys and resolved to go down there to sort things out once and for all. Altogether, there must have been about two hundred of us, all trooping down there to face off against them, and I was right at the front. Even though I'd never scrapped, I'm a big lad, so I was confident I'd be able to look after myself if it came down to it. In my head, I thought I was on some noble mission to save the school's honour. We walked around a corner, and spotted these four Chinese lads that had been causing all the trouble. Part of me expected them to run when they saw us. But nope, the opposite happened. One of them jumped up and started coming towards us, and I saw he had a lump of wood in each hand. At the time I had a record bag for school, so I held that up as if it was a battering ram. So now we were both tooled up. It was going down. These four mental-looking Chinese lads were coming right at us. So I stopped, and took off my record bag. Then, I swear down, I heard a voice say to me, 'B, turn around.' It was like divine intervention or something.

I turned around, and realised that I was completely alone. All two hundred of these kids that had been behind me seconds earlier had run off down the road and left me on my own! So there I was, outnumbered four-to-one. I remember thinking that if I ran, people would see me and my image would suffer. But then my survival instincts kicked in and I broke into a sprint. A glass Oasis bottle went whizzing past my head. I ran so fast I raced past the other two hundred boys shouting, 'Where do you lot think you're going?'

Next thing I know, someone's called the police and I'm in a room back at the school being interviewed. It was mainly for my own protection I think, because they'd heard that the Triads were after my blood. After forty minutes or so, everyone had dispersed so they let me go. But that wasn't the end of it. When I was walking home with two of my mates, I saw a glimpse of a black puffa jacket pop around the corner and then go back in. I knew then something was up. It turned out the four Chinese lads, all of whom were older, had been waiting for us the whole time. They were deadly serious. So I shouted, 'Run!' and the three of us just legged it. I remember thinking after, that's twice in the same day I'd run from the same boys! About a year later I saw one of them on the train by himself. I was going to beat him up just for making me run a couple of times, but in the end I let it go. I didn't need the hassle.

Anyone who knew me when I was growing up will tell you that for me, girls were always second to football. I didn't lose my virginity until I was sixteen, and didn't even start noticing girls until around then. They only came into play when it was dark. Not for the reasons you might think, but just because you couldn't play football in the dark. I had game, and didn't even know it at the time. People say I'm a likeable character, and people gravitate toward me. I'm charismatic. Even from a young age, I just thought talking to females was a natural thing to do. It felt good. I wasn't doing it with any kind of agenda, though it didn't take me long to realise that to get anywhere with the ladies you have to tell them what they want to hear. It was the same concept I came to adopt later when I talked to football managers. You have to tell them what they want to hear, and keep it minimal. Don't overdo it or they'll know you're bullshitting them. The biggest mistake a lot of guys make is they underestimate both women and managers. Don't.

The only aspect I had a problem with was breaking the ice. For the life of me, I didn't know how to just go up to a girl and introduce myself. It wasn't like I wasn't confident. I was fucking confident! But I found that initial hurdle very hard to overcome. It's the pressure of knowing that if you mess that bit up, you have nowhere to go. You're done. To help me in that respect, I came up with this spiel whereby I would tell girls I was in a group and we were casting for a music video. Then I'd ask for their phone number and leave. I was getting numbers left, right and centre! When I called them, I would just go off on a different tangent and not even mention the supposed music video. If it ever did get mentioned, and one of the girls asked me if I could sing, I would just give them a few bars of 'If I Ever Fall in Love' by Shai. That was my go-to song. It usually worked.

There was a girl called Hannah who went to Highgate Wood school. She had these beautiful hazel eyes. We all used to hang out in Wood Green. She would be with her crew, and I would be with mine. One day my friend Marlon, who was a bit of a player, went up to them and asked for her number. For some reason she didn't give it up on the day, but I saw her a while after and she was like, 'Here's my number, give it to your friend.' I thought, 'Nah, that's not going to happen,' and later I called her myself. This was before mobiles, so we were talking house phone to house phone. I would wait until my parents went to sleep, and I would call her. We would talk for hours. The phone bill that quarter was about £400. My parents went up the wall. Hannah and I were never going to be a thing in *that* way. She was merely my education on the do's and dont's with a young female.

All the best players from the four rival schools – Highbury Grove, Holloway, Central Foundation and St Aloysius – came together to play for the district team. First it was Islington, then it became Islington & Camden. We hadn't lost a game in five years. I couldn't get into the team as a forward, so I played centre-back. There was so much talent there. As well as Joe Cole there was John Halls (Stoke City, Reading, Brentford), Jay Murray (Leyton Orient, Chelmsford), Mehmet Unal (Wimbledon, Clyde) and a few other names. It was star-studded from front to back. I remember Joe Cole scoring a cracking goal for the district team. The keeper came out and he nonchalantly flicked the ball over his head and it dropped into the net. It was the kind of goal I was scoring for fun, all the time, but I wasn't getting the same kind of hoopla as Joe was. I clapped the goal, but that was the first time I remember feeling a pang of jealousy. Not because Joe was the one who'd scored, but because of all the attention and adulation he was getting for doing it. But obviously, as I was playing centre-back I wasn't getting the opportunities. I wasn't there to score goals. It was my job to stop them being scored at the other end.

Sometimes I hated training with the district team. The thing that I always loved most about football was how pure it was.

It was all about fun. Football is a game at the end of the day, and that's the whole point of games. It was escapism. But with the district set-up, I felt that some fathers forged a relationship with the manager just to get their sons in the team. The manager would always put his mate's boys first, regardless of how good they were or how well they were playing. It was so contrived. That was my first experience with politics in football, and it was the only place I ever played where I didn't wholeheartedly enjoy the game. So I played for a little while, then I left of my own accord.

When I was fifteen, I signed for the St Mary's Youth Club team in Islington. This was the side who'd beaten my eight-a-side estate team the year before with Shaun Wright-Phillips playing for them. When our estate team folded, all the best players were poached by St Mary's Youth Club so they took me and Arhan, our midfield Xavi. They had good pedigree. As well as Shaun, John Halls and Gifton Noel-Williams had played for them, and the club made history by being the first club to win the London Youth Cup three years in a row. That was a good competition to win. When I signed, the manager was a man called Nick Adams. He was a bit of a local legend, and had helped set the place up back in 1977. In the early days St Mary's was mainly known for football, but it did a lot for the local community beyond that. They had workshops covering a range of things, not just football. DJ Spoony came through it, along with Leona Lewis and Alexandra Burke. Nick Adams was a great man manager. He was so good at instilling confidence and belief in people. He told me I was as good as, if not better than, any other player he had ever seen. To a fifteen-year-old, that means a lot.

One season we travelled up to enter the Umbro Manchester Tournament, with Blackburn Rovers, Manchester United, Bolton Wanderers and a couple of other big teams. It was eleven-a-side, Under-16s. Because of the quality of the opposition, nobody gave us much of a chance. But we went there and won the whole thing. We beat the team who knocked out Blackburn in the semi 6-3 in the final. I remember a group of us standing around before the game and hearing all about this big, intimidating centre-back they had. He was supposed to be a real bully. Kicking everyone about and just knocking them out of the game. I couldn't wait to get stuck into him. They had the ball for the kick-off, but there was some kind of delay so for a full thirty seconds I was just standing there eyeballing this defender. I didn't break eye contact once. It got to the point where his whole team were looking around at us wondering what the problem was. It definitely rattled them. The game finally kicked off and I ran straight at this defender like a bull out of the gate. He didn't even have the ball! After that, he was broken. He had a terrible game. So it's probably true what boxers say about the fight being won in the stare-down. That was when I learned that getting your mind right before a game is just as important as playing it. I took that with me throughout my whole career. Something else I learned quickly was that the ones banging the walls and screaming at each other to psyche themselves up are fake. Everyone gets prepared in their own way, but the too-loud ones are usually only putting on a facade for anybody who happens to be watching. We were a sick team and won that final at a canter. After the tournament, Manchester United scouted six of our players and Bolton scouted another three. Our performances down there were big news in the area at the time, so much so that we made the *Islington Gazette*.

Shortly after the tournament, the St Mary's manager, Nick, got a call from an Arsenal scout who said he would get in trouble if he missed a player from Highbury Grove who ended up at their great rivals Manchester United so he asked me to go down there for a trial, more as a favour to him than anything else. They had Jay Bothroyd there at the time, a very good player. I went down there, played a game, and scored. I remember looking around at the players, and the facilities, and thinking, 'Wow. This is Arsenal!' They were Premier League standard, a cut above most of the other clubs I'd had dealings with up until then. Everything was top notch. It didn't get much better than that.

Arsenal were impressed with me, and asked me to go back for a second week. I was told they very rarely did that, so there was potential for something to happen there. At the same time, however, I got a call from Bolton saying they wanted to have a look at me as well. The Gunners were challenging for the Premier League title and had a cracking squad full of internationals, so there obviously wouldn't be many opportunities around the first team for at least a couple of years. But Bolton were yo-yoing between the top two divisions and seemed to be in a permanent state of flux. I thought I'd be able to break through there faster. So me and a couple of other lads from St Mary's went up there and did well collectively. We played two games together, and I think I scored in both. To me, these were just games. I can't remember even getting nervous beforehand. I was like, 'This is football, man! This is what I love doing.' I knew a couple of the other lads in the team so I wasn't up there by myself and I felt comfortable. I didn't really feel any pressure.

I was confident of making a big impression at Bolton. I thought they were my kind of club. But then the manager and all the backroom staff suddenly got fired and we were just four lads from London who nobody knew about. So that fizzled out, leaving only the Arsenal option. But then to make it even worse, Nick pulled me to one side and said, 'Look, once you turn down

Arsenal, there's no going back to them.' So that was that and I had to move on.

When I was in my mid-to-late teens, going to football trials at different clubs was like a fashion statement. Because I had so many mates into football, it seemed like everyone was doing it. I remember turning up to them not knowing anyone, and just trying to look after myself and play my own game. If there's a pass on, pass the ball. If there's a shot on, shoot. I never felt out of my depth, but the rejection side of it was hard. It was embarrassing at times. Whenever I went for a trial, I used to tell my family and mates about it. And then if nothing came of it, I'd have to go back and tell them what had happened.

Around this time, I played for Leicester City on trial against Aston Villa and we got hammered 6-1. They had Gareth Barry and Darius Vassell, two future England players, up front. Vassell was ridiculously fast, and Barry ran the whole show. He looked so composed on the ball. I remember the Leicester manager, Martin O'Neill, telling me that was the standard I had to be at if I wanted to play for his club. I remember thinking, 'How?' I wasn't in the professional set-up. I'd never been given the chance. Give me top-level coaches and let me train with international players every day, and you'll see improvement. But without those things I could only be the player I was. That really got to me. He was comparing me to someone like Darius Vassell, who was a completely different kind of player, and leaps and bounds ahead of anyone else anyway. A few years later he would become one of the best forwards in the country. It was an impossibly high standard.

I had other trials at Oldham Athletic and Crystal Palace which nothing came of. I think a lot of it was about my size. I'm quite unorthodox-looking for a footballer. Maybe it was a bit off-putting for them. Often when you go on trials, the clubs already have a very fixed idea of the kind of player they want, and if you don't fit into that little box they won't be interested. My fitness was something else that was mentioned a couple of times. But to me, that was something we could work on. If these managers and coaches were used to working with boys who train every day, then they meet someone who doesn't, of course there's going to be a noticeable difference.

I'll be the first to admit that I didn't always do myself justice. I went for yet another trial at Luton Town. I don't know what it was with that particular one. It wasn't that I thought I was too good. Maybe I just couldn't be arsed with it. There were a lot of boys there, and I was playing the second half of a game. I was getting ready, and the manager said to me, 'Are you going to play with that ring on?'

I said, 'Well, no. I'll take it off before I go on.' Then I sat on the bench to watch the first half with my headphones on.

A minute later there was a tap on my shoulder. The manager again. 'Are you really going to sit there and listen to music?'

I eventually got on, and played left wing. It was an easy game for me. I was cutting inside and linking play. I'd gone up there with Nick from St Mary's, and on the drive back he said that the Luton manager had told him I had an attitude problem. I remember thinking, 'Well, whatever . . .'

Maybe that was the point I started getting a bit discouraged, but even then I never really doubted myself. I never thought for a moment that it wasn't going to happen for me. I always knew I would be playing football for a living in some shape or form. But I did think, 'Hang on, I'm getting knocked back quite a bit now.' But there are two ways you can take rejection. You can either dwell on it and let it drag you down, or you can use it as fuel for the fire and let it spur you on, so that's what I tried to do. Football anywhere is ultra-competitive, but it's even more so in London. It's the centre of the football universe. When I was younger, nobody ever told me I wasn't good enough. If anything, it was the opposite and people were telling me I was too good. I've thought since that maybe a bit of complacency set in, or maybe I didn't turn it on at the right times, or say the right things to the right people. That, combined with the

OSD in my knees I was dealing with at the time, was enough to trip me up.

• • •

A couple of months before I left Highbury Grove, I moved out of the estate and over to Walthamstow. It was a big life change. I'd only ever lived on the estate, and we were a close-knit group of lads. The estate boys. I didn't do very well in my GCSEs. When I took my results home and showed my parents, they weren't even surprised. They were adamant that my brothers and my sister were all going to get good results so they could get into university, but they didn't even try pushing me too hard in that direction because they knew I was too into football.

After I moved to Walthamstow, I did a business studies course at Waltham Forest College for a year. That was my mother's doing. She told me I either had to sign a contract with a club, or stay in school. It was that simple. So I signed up at college for a year just to buy some time and keep her happy really. I had no intention of ever getting a career in business at the time, though I would put what I learned there to good use in the future. It was worse for me because all my mates from school had gone to the City and Islington College, which was just up the road from the school. But by the time I applied there were no places left because I didn't plan on even going to college. Waltham Forest was easier for me to get to. It was just up the road. But again, I didn't know anyone there. Just my luck. I was going to all these trials by myself where I didn't know anybody, and when I wasn't doing that I would go to school, where again, I didn't know anybody. I did feel isolated at times. I think a lot of teenagers feel like that when they're trying to find their place in the world. You just have to believe in your own ability, work hard, push on and find something that appeals to you.

By then, it had been decided that I was far too good for the St Mary's Under-16 side, so at the age of just sixteen I started playing for the men's side on Wednesday nights. DJ Spoony used to turn out for them. I remember going with Nick to watch a game and saying to their striker, a bald-headed fella, 'I'm here to take your place, mate.' The whole changing room just erupted. I meant it in a jokey way, but they were probably all thinking, 'Who's this little kid who thinks he can come in here and start saying shit like that?'

I was as confident then as I am now. It didn't matter to me whether I was playing against men or boys. I felt I could handle any situation. Eight or nine of the players were black, so it was a real rootsy east London team. We had a white midfielder, but he knew how to hang with the brothers. It was a tight group of lads. I was on the bench for the next game, and I got on the pitch and scored. When the bald-headed striker saw that, he never came back. I ended up playing two up front with a guy called Tyrone Husbands. He went to Highbury Grove as well, but he was three or four years older than me so our paths never crossed at school. He was a good player, and he also had trials at Arsenal and one or two others, I think. He was another one of those gifted players who fall through the cracks.

I was warming up for a game one night when this black guy came up to me and introduced himself as Gary. He said, 'Look, I'm an agent. I've been watching you, and really I feel I can help take your career to the next level.'

You could tell by looking at him that this guy had money. He wore designer clothes, lived in Elephant & Castle, and drove a Ferrari. So I was looking at him thinking that whatever this guy did, he was good at it. I was only too happy to get to know him. It turned out he wasn't just a football agent. He was kind of an entrepreneur, and more into building projects. He would look for raw talent in whatever field, then make the necessary investments and nurture it. He was pretty innovative. I was doing a bit of singing at the time, and when he heard that, he was like, 'Okay, these two things you're into, football and singing, we're gonna fuse them together.'

As a kid who'd just turned seventeen, I found it amazing that

I'd found someone who had that much faith in me. So when I was still at college, I formed a group. It was called 2NBN. Or Too Naughty But Nice. There were five of us, including my brother Yemi. Gary became our manager. He spent over £10,000 on us. He was just throwing money at it. We had flyers made up, choreographers working with us on dance routines, professional photographers. There's still footage on the internet if you look hard enough, though I wouldn't recommend it.

I'm not embarrassed about it, but to be fair we were fucking terrible. We weren't exactly Boys II Men. I'd told Gary I could sing, but the truth was I couldn't sing for shit. I was the dancer of the group. A bit like Bez off the Happy Mondays without the maracas. I was at college at the time, and we did a gig there. We even cut a track called 'Why' and released it on CD. It was a good song, we just weren't a very good group. We did a gig at a pub, where all our deficiencies were cruelly exposed. The whole place nearly kicked off we were so bad. That was proper embarrassing. Poor Gary started out with a Ferrari, and by the end of it he was driving around in a fucking Mini Metro.

Despite growing up on the estate and not having much money, I was never tempted to cross the line into criminality. I haven't got too many bad things to say about the police. Everyone knows they do a difficult job. But there have been a few occasions over the years where I believe I've been unjustifiably singled out. Maybe I'll get pulled over and I think to myself, 'You're blatantly only doing this because I'm black and I'm driving a nice car!'

There have also been times where the police come on to me with an attitude and assume I've been up to no good because I'm a big black guy with money. I've had to explain to them that they don't know who I am or what I do. They don't know where the money came from, so it's wrong of them to make assumptions and snap judgements. So maybe between the size thing and the colour of my skin, I do suffer from discrimination in some ways. Or, at least, I have done in the past. But when people ask me if I've ever encountered out-and-out racism, apart from the odd one-off incident, the answer is no. Not in this country, anyway. Playing abroad, that's a different story.

I get the same thing with security guards at gigs and clubs. They all seem to gravitate toward the big guy, which is understandable, but any man can be walking around with a gun or a knife in his pocket. It's common sense. Me, I don't need to carry weapons. I can look after myself without them. I've actually had people say to me, 'We can't control you because of your size.' Is that my fault? You may as well judge someone for having long hair or a beard. It goes back to those preconceptions, and misconceptions, we all have. When they see a big black guy, a lot of people just jump to conclusions. But there have literally only been a handful of times anything has come of it in all my thirty-five years and when I look at percentages like that, I don't think I've had it too bad. It probably helps that I don't drink when I go out, even when I'm clubbing, so I can always be coherent and reasonable. I didn't have a drink until I was twenty-eight. When I got to thirty, my brothers began asking me whether I was a man or a mouse and insisted on getting me drunk. That didn't take much and it led to a whole world of trouble, which I'll get around to later. Despite my size, I'm a real lightweight. I only need one or two and I'm buzzing.

I've been in a police cell once in my life. What my older brother did for me, I did more for my little brother. I looked out for him. He went to a different school, so whenever he needed me I would be there in a flash. Furthermore, because I was an estate lad, if I had to, I could have eight or ten boys behind me in an instant. We weren't a gang, but to someone who didn't know us, we might've seemed like one.

My little brother Dele is four years younger than me. He was having problems at school with boys a year or two older, and it was a pretty big deal to him. Of course, those boys were still younger than me. There was one incident where he called me down to his school because some kid was threatening him. So about seven of us went down there, and one of my brother's friends headbutted the kid and laid him out. The police were called, and the kid pointed the finger at me so the police arrested me and three other boys. That's how I ended up in a cell. I was in there for eight hours, and I just remember thinking, 'Please don't tell my mum!' She would have gone mental on us both. It was a case of being in the wrong place at the wrong time, but because I hadn't done anything they let me go and nothing came of it.

I never felt out of place when I went on trials at established professional clubs. But after the Bolton fiasco, the first trial I had that I actually thought might lead somewhere was at Watford. I was seventeen, and it came about through Gifton Noel-Williams. By this time, I had a good sense of what was expected at a trial. You have to do something that they'll remember you by, but you don't go out and try to beat four men. It's not needed and by trying to do too much you invariably fail and end up just making yourself look stupid.

At the time, I was still under contract with St Mary's. Nick, who was now like my unofficial agent, was a little hustler. In fairness, he was primarily a youth worker, and it was all about the kids for him. He did a lot of good things for the community, and channelled it all through the youth club. But funding was limited and money was tight, so he had to always look at ways he could get new equipment. He would persuade young footballers to sign contracts with the youth club as a way of getting the pro or semi-pro clubs they signed for later on to send them kits or balls or something. To this day, I'm not even sure about the specifics, but I think Nick had me signed to a contract under which I was allowed to play only three games for any other club. It was a two-week trial at Watford, which included three scheduled games. So obviously, if they wanted me to play more than those three games, they were going to have to talk business with Nick and pay some form of compensation to get round this contractual problem.

I ended up staying on at Watford, when Jimmy Gilligan was the Under-18s manager there. I would later go on to play with his son Ryan at Northampton Town. Football is a small world. Graham Taylor was the first-team manager at the time, and the club had just been promoted to the Premier League. I remember walking into training in the early days full of bravado and thinking, 'I can do this. No problem!' It felt as if after all the knock-backs and disappointments I was finally kicking on and getting a deserved opportunity to prove myself. I'd signed for a Premier League club.

I would go to meet Gifton Noel-Williams at Finsbury Park in the mornings, and he used to pick me up in his Golf convertible and take me to training in Stanmore. Every time he picked me up I'd think to myself, 'I have to make it, because this is the car I want.' Gifton, being a couple of years older, was just breaking into the first team. I was in the same Under-18s side as Jerel Ifil (Watford, Swindon Town, Aberdeen) and Lloyd Doyley, who went on to be a club legend making well over 300 appearances for the Hornets. They were the two centre-halves. In midfield we had Lee Johnson, who never broke through at Vicarage Road but played at Yeovil Town and Bristol City before forging a successful career in management, and up front was Steve Brooker, who went on to make a name for himself at Port Vale and Bristol City. This was the calibre of player around me. I knew I had to work hard to stay in the team. Even though I knew I could play, I was realistic enough to know that Brooker was better than me. I was still pretty raw, but he had all the tools. There was another forward in the team called Fabien who everyone thought would be the Next Big Thing, but I knew I was better than him and he didn't really enter my thinking too much.

I didn't score in any of the three games I played, but I knew I'd done enough to impress. Even though I couldn't play any more matches, I continued training with the squad every day for six or eight weeks after that. It just became the norm. I felt part of the club. To all intents and purposes, I was a Watford player. While this was going on, Jimmy Gilligan left to take up a role at Nottingham Forest, so Luther Blissett took his place as Under-18s manager. Until then he had been a coach. He wasn't what you would call overly friendly, but he was cool. This was a guy who'd left Watford to play at AC Milan and then come back again, so you couldn't help but admire him and what he'd achieved in the game. He epitomised everything a local hero should be.

One day they lined us up for an eleven-a-side game against Graham Taylor's first team, with Gifton up front, and club captain Rob Page (Watford, Sheffield United and Wales) at the back. I remember the ball came up to me and I headed it down the line, palmed off Page who'd gone for it, and cut the ball back across the goal. I made him look stupid, and I took a lot of confidence from that. I remember someone saying, 'Check his passport. There's no way he's only seventeen!'

I'd just left college, so being at Watford felt like the next step in a natural progression. I still wasn't getting paid, but my outgoings weren't much. I wasn't driving and I was still living at home. I was getting lifts to the club, and eating lunch there. It wasn't like I needed much spending money. I was just happy learning my trade and doing something I loved every day. I made a little bit of money on the side teaching dance a couple of nights a week at the youth club. They were very much into music production. Heartless Crew came from there, among others, and dance was a by-product of that. I was basically a youth worker. Despite 2NBN coming to nothing, I was still bang into my music at that stage. I did some routines with Alexandra Burke and a few others.

However, after a couple of months at Watford, I got into a rut and my discipline started to waver a bit. I began going out clubbing, and there were times when Gifton would come to pick me up at Finsbury Park and I'd still be in bed sleeping. That happened a couple of times, and then the third time he said, 'B, I kid you not, I'm not picking you up any more. You're taking the piss. I get you in here, I even come to pick you up, and you can't even be bothered to get out of bed.' So then I started taking the train into training. It made things a bit harder for me, but I still wasn't paying because back then there was no ticket barrier at either Walthamstow or Stanmore station.

Around this time, David Hockaday replaced Luther Blissett as Watford Under-18s manager. One day he told me that he wanted to have a meeting with me and my parents. Those kinds of meetings in football are either really good or really bad, and I honestly didn't know which way this one would go. I remember wearing a shirt and tie, and my parents both taking a day off work to go. When we got there, we all had to sit there and listen to this guy say, 'We have eight strikers all trying to get into one team, so we're not going to offer you anything. I don't think you're of the right calibre to push on from here.'

I always take rejection with a smile. It's a part of life, and it won't do you any good to beat yourself up over it. You just have to take it on the chin and move on. But right then all I could think about was my parents taking time off work for that. It still gripes me to this day. I was of age by then; Hockaday could have had a quiet word with me. There was no need to have a sit-down meeting. But even then the guy wasn't finished. He said, 'Do I think you're going to make it at the very top? No, I don't. Do I think you can forge some kind of career in football? Maybe.'

So I said, 'Yeah, fair enough. But know this, when I come back to Watford and score a hat-trick, I'm going to turn around and smile at you. Thank you very much.'

So that was it, a very unglamorous and undignified end to my stint at my first professional club.

3 TOUGH TIMES ABROAD

FK Atlantas (2000–02)

After Watford, I was at a loose end. My then agent/manager Gary had a Lithuanian wife. And her brother knew a member of the coaching staff at a club called FK Atlantas, so he arranged a trial for me there. Lithuania isn't exactly a footballing superpower. To tell the truth, I didn't even know where it was. I'd never heard of it. But apparently this club had some pedigree. They'd been national champions four times, most recently in 1984, and were regulars in European competition. The name means 'Atlantic Ocean' in Lithuanian. My first reaction was a firm 'no'. Mainly because I knew I was good enough to make it in Britain. I didn't think I needed to go elsewhere to get a start. But Gary persuaded me that I should go over and do the trial because, if nothing else, I could come back and tell British clubs that a European club was interested in me. He said it would be a good bargaining tool. The trip wouldn't even be costing me anything. The club had a bit of money, so they offered to pay for my return flights, meals and accommodation at a nice hotel. I began to look at it as a free holiday, and who doesn't like free holidays?

I didn't have much else going on anyway. I remember around that time I was going out clubbing almost every night. Sunday I'd go to a place called Capital Club, Sound was on a Monday, then Tuesday I'd go to Gas Club, Wednesday was Hanover Grand, Thursday was Samantha's, Friday was Ministry of Sound, Saturday was somewhere else. I'd also slot in the odd visit to Funky Buddha and China White. Back then there was somewhere to go every night. It's not the same now. These days you have a handful of clubs who have monopolised the entire city. I didn't drink, but if you'd seen me dancing, you'd have thought I was the drunkest guy in the club. Music got me on a high. As enjoyable as it was, I knew I had to break that cycle of going out clubbing every night, so eventually I agreed to go to FK Atlantas for a two-week trial. I felt I had nothing to lose. It was a small sacrifice to make for the good of my career.

Around this time, I met Michelle, or Mich, who would become my long-term partner. It was my best mate's birthday, so we went to Corts wine bar. I saw a girl I liked and asked her for her number, but she wouldn't give it to me. Later the same night I saw Mich. I often remind her now that if that first girl had said yes, we probably wouldn't be together today! Because we met when we were so young, Mich and I have virtually grown up together. In the early days we were both going out a lot, so we would only see each other during the week. Then on the weekends, she would go out with her friends and I would go out with mine. We both loved the garage scene and had a lot going on in our social lives.

I found out later that on what was supposed to be our first proper date she wasn't even going to come. She couldn't remember what I looked like. So she did that girl thing where they arrange to have one of their friends call them while they are on a date and give them an excuse to bail if they need one. I remember her phone ringing and her saying to her friend, 'Nah, it's okay.' So I suppose I dodged a bullet there. I took her back to my parents' house and we watched *The Five Heartbeats*, which is a film about the trials and tribulations of a vocal group in America. It's based on groups like the Temptations and the

Drifters. I was hoping to get to this part where I could sing a bit and put some moves on her, but Mich put paid to that about fifteen minutes in by saying, 'What's this rubbish? It's boring as fuck!'

The first time I went to Lithuania I had to travel out on my own, and hook up with a couple of Gary's other players when I got out there. Before I went, I kept imagining the place as being all cold, gloomy and grey. For some reason I kept thinking I was going to Russia. But I got off the plane, and it was hot! My first impressions were that it was a lovely place. It was proper nice. The club president picked me up in an old-school BMW. His name was Arnus. It wasn't hard for him to identify me because I was the only black guy there. It was a four-hour drive to my digs in Klaipėda, the third-largest city in the country, where the club is based. It's not much more than a small port town on the Baltic Sea, which makes it sound really grim, but it's actually quite nice. Klaipėda has been under German rule in the past but was incorporated into Lithuania after a revolt in 1923. These days it's right in the middle of a chain of seaside resorts popular with German tourists and rich Russians.

The hotel we were staying in, set in a nice woodland estate, was lovely. The people were nice and the weather was beautiful. It was idyllic. Even the food, which I soon came to realise can be a bit hit and miss abroad, was okay. Lots of cold meats and salad. I was excited to be there. But, looking back, my first impressions kinda sugar-coated what Lithuania was really like. When you're older, you can see the bigger picture. But when you're eighteen and have barely ever set foot out of the city where you were born, you only have a very limited world view to go from. The only thing I didn't like about those couple of weeks was that the TV was shit. I mean really bad. I'm the kind of guy who needs a TV, especially when I'm away from home. It's a comfort device. The TV in Lithuania only had about four English channels, the best of those being MTV. So I just remember watching *a lot* of music videos. There were times I almost forgot I was there to play football and started looking at the whole thing as a free holiday.

When I went to the club for training, the first thing that hit me was how much better than the other players I was. I know that sounds arrogant, but the standard was really quite low. Despite all the knock-backs I'd had, and even after the Watford debacle, I still had this unwavering confidence. Like most eighteen-year-olds, I thought I could do anything. On the third day of training, we were playing a practice match and the goalkeeper came out to meet me. I just chipped him, and walked back for the restart thinking, 'Yeah, man. That's what I'm about!' It was effortless.

During the whole trial, I was playing well and on a high. I

didn't spend too much time out and about exploring, but I didn't get any negative vibes at all. There was no hint about what was to come. I was just thinking I should take it for what it is, and make the most of it. I thought I'd just be doing the two weeks, and then saying my goodbyes. The Lithuanian season finishes in November anyway, which was only a couple of months away. It's too cold to play during the winter, with the average temperature in January dropping to around –7°C.

So I did the trial, went home, and some time later I got a call from Gary. He was like, 'They liked what they saw, and they wanna sign you for three years.'

I couldn't believe it. Three years? He said their new season started the following April, and they wanted me back in Lithuania by the March.

It's every eighteen-year-old baller's dream to sign a professional contract. Especially for a club with the stature and pedigree of FK Atlantas. But three years in Lithuania? That quickly became my back-up option. I had six months or so to find a club in the UK, which I thought would become easier once everyone knew I had the option of going to a European club who would be playing UEFA Europa League football the following season. In the meantime, I went back to St Mary's, and immediately Nick was like, 'Right. If you do sign with them, tell them we want them to send us twenty-one kits and six new balls!'

I had my first boys' holiday that December. Me, my brother, and a few other lads went to New York for a week. It was freezing. I called Mich, and she screamed down the phone in excitement. It was the best feeling. Until then, she'd been doing the girl thing and acting cool. Even when I called her from Lithuania she didn't seem that bothered. Talking to her afterwards, she said she'd never meant to react that way. It was just natural. That was the time when I started to realise that this girl was missing me when I was away. I began to think that maybe something could happen with her. But obviously, not if I was playing football in Lithuania. It made the prospect even less attractive.

Christmas came and went, February rolled around, and I began to wonder why I hadn't had any more trials. Not a single one. I talked to Gary and he was like, 'Yeah, sorry B. I'm trying, but nobody's biting.'

Looking back, I'm sure he was being genuine, but at the same time, because he knew he had the FK Atlantas deal in the bank, maybe he wasn't trying as hard to get me trials as he would have otherwise. In the end he told me to make a decision, because they wanted me out there by March. The club were offering me US$3,000 cash-in-hand a week, plus accommodation and free flights back to London whenever I wanted. I didn't want to sign for three years, so I convinced Gary to get me a year with another year's option. At least, I thought I did.

The moment the plane landed in Lithuania that second time, it was a totally different feeling. There was snow everywhere and it was freezing cold. What the fuck? I hate the cold. I'm just not built for it. A driver met me at the airport and took me to Klaipėda. The chairman, who used to be a goalkeeper for the club, obviously knew some people in high places. He would park his jeep anywhere, knowing that nobody would dare give him a ticket. He looked a bit like Peter Schmeichel with a goatee, and couldn't speak a word of English. I sat down with him and Arnus, the club president, and signed a contract. Except I didn't read through it thoroughly. This was all new to me. I'd left all the negotiating to Gary and just assumed I'd get the year with another year's option that I asked for.

After I signed, I went to the apartment where I was staying and put the telly on. This time even the telly was different. I'd been at a hotel before, which obviously catered for a lot of international guests. This was an apartment in a suburban area. There were only about six channels, and none of them was English. I couldn't even get MTV. So the next day I saw Arnus and told him that if he didn't sort my telly out, get me a satellite dish or something, I was going home. It was that simple. I didn't give a shit about the contract. If I get something in my head, it's getting done. I've always been the same. He must have sensed I was serious, so he took me to a shop in the town, and we arranged some kind of system where we had a top-up card, and that gave us a few extra channels.

I lived with this Japanese guy called Bob, another one of Gary's players. Bob wasn't his real name, obviously, it was a nickname he had because nobody could pronounce his real name. Bob was a born traveller. He'd already lived in a few different countries, spoke fluent English, and before long was speaking decent Lithuanian as well, which was admirable. Lithuanian is a difficult language. I remember thinking, 'Fuck that.' Even if I spent time studying it, I didn't think I'd be there long enough for it to pay dividends, so I just memorised a few key phrases like, 'Pass' and 'Give me the ball.' I only needed the essentials.

Because I had no telly for the first week or two, I was listening to a lot of music. My Sony Discman went everywhere with me, and my CD of the time was Mario's first album. What a debut. I listened to a lot of R. Kelly as well. Looking back, I had a pretty boring existence, and football was my only release. Just my being there was a big deal in the media. I was the first black player in the history of the Lithuanian league. I'd been in the *Islington Gazette* a few times, but this was a whole new level. It's a small country compared to some, with a population of about 2.9 million, but they are as passionate as any other. I was fending off interview requests left, right and centre.

Obviously, not being able to understand the lingo meant that I couldn't understand any of the press coverage I was getting anyway, so someone else would have to translate and read it to me. It was very surreal.

Bob and I shared a one-bedroom apartment, but the living room doubled as an extra bedroom, and that was mine. It was so close to the stadium, we could walk it. At first, I wasn't feeling any animosity from the locals. I knew I stood out. I was a massive black guy. I stood out everywhere. Even in London. But it wasn't an issue at all. Not in the beginning, anyway.

My teammates were all cordial enough. Well, mostly. There was one I didn't take to. It was obvious he was racist from the outset. He just didn't like me and wasn't at all worried about giving off those kinds of vibes. If I could go back now I'd punch him up. But being so young, and in a strange place, back then I just bit my tongue. There was only one player apart from Bob that spoke any English so I had hardly any conversations with anyone. I had a habit of saying, 'What's up?' so my nickname at the club soon became Zugali, which is Lithuanian for rabbit. It was supposed to be a take on Bugs Bunny, because he was always saying, 'What's up, Doc?'

We drove to our first pre-season game, which was played on Astroturf, and there was snow everywhere. As we were pulling in to the ground I was thinking, 'The game's off. There's no way we can play in this.' But to my astonishment, all the guys on the team trooped off the coach and started warming up in these sub-zero temperatures. This is one of the very few times in my career where I've acted like a diva. I was like, 'Nah, man. I'm not getting off the bus. Fuck that.' So I sat and watched the game from the coach, my headphones on, frozen stiff, thinking, 'What the fuck have I done? This isn't the way it's supposed to be!'

The next pre-season game was an away derby in Klaipėda. It was nothing crazy. Actually, it was quite low-key compared to British football. The attendance was only 500 or so. I remember seeing the fans all standing around the pitch, mingling together in little groups, and I didn't know which fans were ours. There was the odd scarf with club colours on, but because it was so cold everyone was wearing huge winter coats. The game kicked off, and I made a run toward the corner flag. That's when I first heard it. Monkey chants. I had to check myself. I thought they must just be booing me, the new guy, and I was misinterpreting things. But then I realised there was no mistake, they were being mad racist. Blatantly racist. So I played forty-five minutes, then I came off and while the game was still going on I grabbed the president's phone and rang my brother Yemi to tell him about it. I said I'd had enough and wanted to go home. I remember what he told me almost word for word. 'I would never tell you to stay somewhere you don't want to be,' he said. 'But if you cut your losses and come home early, it means they win and you can't let that happen because it will haunt you for ever.'

I went back to my apartment, shut the door, and sulked a bit. Then I woke up the next day with the mentality that nobody runs me out of anywhere. I decided to knuckle down and ride it out. It was one thing my brother saying it, but something else entirely when I said it to myself. If I left and went back to England, it would mean the racists would win. However, if what happened in the next game had happened in the first, I would definitely have just thought 'Fuck it' and left.

Our next game was at Central Stadium, our home ground. When full, it had a capacity of 4,400, but as we were still in pre-season it wasn't even close to full. I came out to warm up, and I immediately heard, 'Zigga zigga zigga, shoot the fucking nigger.' That's a long way from being called a fat Eddie Murphy or someone shouting my tits are offside. So at half-time, I went into the changing room and asked the FK Atlantas captain, who'd played in Poland at quite a high level and spoke reasonable English, what 'Zigga' meant. I thought it was a Lithuanian word. But the captain said it didn't mean anything, they were just using it to rhyme with nigger. He didn't try to dress it up in any way. He just threw it out there and looked me right in the eye. I was still in the mindset that I wasn't going to let them win. So we went out for the second half, and the moment the fans saw me the chants started up again, 'Zigga zigga zigga, shoot the fucking nigger.'

This time, I looked around to see where it was coming from, and noticed that most of the hardcore fanatics were congregating behind one of the goals. They all wore Doc Martens with the jeans tucked in and big puffa jackets. They were the ones chanting. And then I realised, they were FK Atlantas supporters. I was being racially abused by my own fans in my own stadium! That made it ten times worse. It's one thing being abused by away supporters, but something else entirely when your own fans do it to you. I was thinking to myself, 'Hang on, I'm on your side!' I got substituted after an hour, and that brought probably the biggest cheer of the whole game.

The next day, I was called into a meeting with the club president and the chairman. The chairman owned a security company, and he asked me if I wanted a security detail to look after me when I went to the shops and stuff. I was like, 'What? Why?' Even with the chanting, I didn't feel intimidated or scared. Angry, shocked and disappointed. But never intimidated or scared. So I said, 'No, I don't want a security detail.' It wasn't like I was going out raving all the time anyway. I only ever went to the cinema and the supermarket near my apartment.

In many ways, the Lithuanian league was similar to the Scottish league. There were two teams, Kaunas and Žalgiris Vilnius, who were like Rangers and Celtic and always battling it out for first and second, then Atlantas and one or two others were in the little group below them. We were like the equivalent of Aberdeen or Motherwell. Despite all the abuse, I was playing pretty well. I can't remember who I scored my first goal against, I just remember it being a worldy. It whistled into the net. The only game I really struggled in was when we played Žalgiris Vilnius at home, historically the most successful club in the country. They had a pair of huge, imposing centre-halves, who I couldn't get any change out of the entire game. We ended up losing by the odd goal, so even then we weren't outclassed.

That evening, I popped out to the shops. I saw a young girl there. She must have been eleven or twelve years old, and was dressed like a goth. Head to foot in black with the dark eyeliner and everything. She walked right up to me and said, 'White power,' and walked off. I was stunned. Nobody in London would dream of saying something like that, let alone a little girl. I looked around and saw a big group of people in the shop all dressed the same way as her. I don't know if they had put her up to it, or if she came up of her own volition, but I guess her parents must have been there. She was too young to be out by herself. I just glared at them, paid for my stuff, and walked out shaking my head. The reason that incident sticks in my head is because it crossed a boundary. Instead of shouting abuse from a crowd, the girl came up, got right in my personal space, and disrespected me to my face. That was out of order.

The racism was so prevalent, it became the norm. It's a terrible thing to say, but I started to accept it and think, 'Well, this is my life now.' It all stemmed from ignorance. There were just no black people in Lithuania. It's not exactly a culturally diverse place. At least, it wasn't in 2001. The funny thing is, I was never racially abused by any opposition players. We used to tussle all the time, but none of them ever crossed the line. But there was one time when a player on my own team had a go. It was an away game, so there were a couple of thousand people watching. He wanted me to pass to him, but there was no way I could so I kept the ball, and I heard him say, 'Negro.' I went up to him and got in his face in the middle of the match. I didn't give a fuck. So we're arguing, but he's shouting in Lithuanian and I'm shouting back in English. I was going, 'Say that shit again and I'll break your face!' but he didn't understand. It was the most pointless argument ever.

There were a few other occasions where I'd catch the odd word and think it was a bit suspect. I heard my teammate I'd suspected at the start of being racist say a few things, and I'd catch him giving me dirty looks. But I'd never know how much was a genuine cause for concern, and how much was a result of my growing paranoia. What made things worse was that I knew this guy used to hang with the Doc Martens brigade from behind the goal. I used to see them together. It was so hard not knowing the language, and it affected virtually every aspect of my life. If we were losing at half-time, the manager would come into the changing room berating us, pointing fingers and barking orders at people. I'd just be looking at him wondering what the fuck he was saying. There was no interpreter, and it wasn't like he was using diagrams or tactics boards to help the international boys along. He was just ranting in Lithuanian.

I'm not going to lie, it's tough being that age and being away from home. Every day after training I would go to the local Internet cafe and spend about two hours in there chatting on MSN Messenger. That became my main pastime. Laptops were so expensive then, the average person couldn't really afford one. I was saving as much money as I could, but there was still no way I could get one. It was a huge boost to my morale when May rolled around and Mich and my little brother Dele came out to visit for a week. My brother was fourteen, and going to Stoke Newington school at the time. Me and my other brother Yemi could see the direction he was going in, and some of the people he was hanging around with, and knew that if we didn't intervene he was going to go left and maybe take the wrong path. So I asked him and Mich to come out. I thought it would be a new experience, and help open his eyes a little bit.

I thought at one point Mich wasn't going to be able to make it because her passport had expired. But I had to go to the airport to meet Dele and this other young boy Gary was sending out for a trial. I was so relieved when Mich turned up too. Later that day, I took her and my brother to the shop near my apartment to get some snacks and things. The moment we walked in, everyone just stopped what they were doing and stared at us. I had grown accustomed to that kind of treatment by then, and some of the locals had probably grown accustomed to seeing me around. But seeing three black people together? That was a different story. The locals probably thought it was a full-blown invasion or something. This kind of treatment affected my brother, and he started getting his back up. He was looking around going, 'What's everyone looking at?'

He'd never experienced anything like that before, and I had to explain to him that it was normal behaviour for the locals. It wasn't nice, but it was harmless. If you could read the looks on people's faces, most of the time it was more curiosity than animosity. They'd just never seen real live black people before. That incident aside, the rest of the week was amazing. It was so good that after Mich and my brother went back to London I started getting homesick, and a couple of weeks later I stormed into the president's office and told him I was going home for two weeks. It wasn't up for discussion. I wasn't asking for leave. I was telling him I was going.

That first season we were already in the qualifying stages of the Europa League, where we played Rapid Bucharest over two legs in the first round. They'd only narrowly lost to Liverpool the year before, so we knew they were a tasty side. They beat us 4-1 at home. I came on and injured my ankle. It was nothing serious, but ordinarily it would keep me out for a couple of matches. But this was European football, the pinnacle of their career for many footballers, and I wanted to play. The medical staff told me that to have any chance of being involved, I would need an injection for the pain. I said, 'Cool. Do it.' That was the first pain injection I had. It wouldn't be the last.

When we played the away leg, I'd never experienced anything like it before. We had a private jet to Romania, rocked up to the stadium, and there must have been 50,000 fans there. I remember walking onto the pitch thinking, 'Wow. This is amazing. This is what football is all about.' The good vibes didn't last, though. They ended up thrashing us 8-0 on the day. It was men against boys. As a striker I remember being marooned up front watching all the action unfold at the other end. I felt powerless, knowing I couldn't leave my post up top to help out the defence because I was the only outlet. Games like that are the most frustrating thing to have to endure, but they happen and you have to deal with it.

Off the back of that Europa League experience, we went on a good Lithuanian Cup run. At that time, the club hadn't won a trophy in over a decade. All through the run, I wasn't too bothered about winning games. I didn't have that single-minded focus. I just wanted to play football and get paid. But when we got to the final against Žalgiris and I caught sight of the trophy at the side of the pitch, something clicked in my head. I wanted to hold that silverware so bad I was willing to run through walls to get my hands on it. As it happened, I had one of my best games for FK Atlantas and managed to bang in the winner, a sublime volley. We ended up winning the game 1-0. That was a special moment, and remains one of the high-points of my career. It was the biggest trophy I'd ever won. By then I'd bought into the whole Zugali thing, so whenever I scored my celebration would be a bunny hop. That just made the experience even more bizarre.

When the ref blew the final whistle, all our fans ran onto the pitch. For a few moments I got so caught up in the moment I lost my bearings. It was pure elation. When I came to my senses, I looked around and all I could see were skinheads with their tops off showing swastika tattoos. Hundreds of them. Then, for the first time since I'd been in the country, I started to feel uneasy. Someone could hit me with something in the midst of it all, or even stab me. They could disappear into the crowd never to be seen again, and I'd be going down. Very quickly, I went from elation to edginess. It could all have turned very nasty, but luckily for me the skinheads were in a good mood. There's a picture showing the team crouching down with the cup, and behind us all you can see is all these skinheads. I'm in there somewhere, as far away from the skinheads as I could get.

In the aftermath of the cup final win, everything changed. Suddenly, we were being treated like A-listers. The chairman took us to this fancy hotel for a big celebration where Bob and I were coerced into singing an R. Kelly track for the team; we met the mayor of Klaipėda; no restaurant we ate in for weeks after would let us pay for anything; a new store opened and they asked me to cut the ribbon. I was a proper celebrity. I still used to get racist chants on away trips, but the Klaipėda racists were well and truly pacified. They loved me after my cup final goal. Oxide & Neutrino had a track out at the time called 'Up Middle Finger'. That became my anthem. After the difficult start, there were two things I wanted to accomplish. I wanted to achieve something during my time in Lithuania, and I wanted to silence the racists. As it happened, I fulfilled both ambitions with just one kick of the ball.

I had every intention to leave the club and go back to the UK at the end of my first season. To finish on such a high would have been a nice way to do it. So I asked my agent/manager Gary to find me another club. That was when he dropped the bombshell that the contract I'd signed wasn't for a year with another year's option at all, it was for a full three years. I could have killed him, but I was more angry with myself. I should have read the small print. Another thing was that because I was being paid in cash, the contract stipulated I wouldn't get paid for the close season between November and March because obviously I wouldn't be there to collect it. Instead, they would keep it for me until I went back. I think that could have been a cunning way to ensure that foreign players honoured their contracts. I didn't mind too much about not getting paid for that couple of months. I'd saved a bit of money by then and I was back living with my parents in London, but it wasn't the ideal scenario.

As a little bonus, at the end of my first season we finished second in the league, ahead of Žalgiris on goal difference. That ensured us Europa League football again, where we again went out in the qualifying round, this time to the Bulgarian team Litex, who beat us 8-1 on aggregate. Probably as a result of winning the Lithuanian Cup, Bob and I were moved to a bigger apartment. This one was plush! I had my own bedroom, and, best of all, we were able to negotiate a satellite dish. I commandeered the TV and put it in my room because Bob was more into reading. One of my mates came out on trial during the pre-season. I sorted that out and made sure the club paid for everything. In the end they didn't offer him terms, but it was nice to have some company for a few weeks. We would go out and about, and I generally felt much better about life.

The club brought in a commercial guy, who'd been working in basketball over in America. Basketball is huge in Lithuania. It's probably their number one sport. Because I had a bit of a name by that point, they planned on using me for marketing purposes. They bumped my weekly salary up, but said I would be able to go back to England only once during the entire season. That was never going to work because I'd already planned one trip home and wasn't about to make that the only one. They weren't happy about it because the season was just starting, but I made up some excuse and went back to London anyway. When I returned to Lithuania, I took my brother Yemi out with me because I didn't want to go on my own. There's a photo of us going around from when we arrived and we look like the Mitchell brothers off *EastEnders*. He's wearing a white T-shirt, I'm wearing a black one.

When I got back, the club started making this big thing in the media about how fit I looked. They were saying I looked trim, sharp, and how ready I was for the new season. The commercial guy had arranged a tournament in Klaipėda with us and a few other teams, and my brother came along. It was like a big publicity thing, so there were loads of local and national media there. My brother hadn't played football for a long time, and I was afraid he was going to embarrass himself, and, at the same time, embarrass me. I wasn't sure if he'd be able to handle it, so I told him not to go on. I don't think I ever told him the real reason why. I did feel like a dickhead afterwards. He had my back enough times when we were growing up. I should have put a bit of faith in him in that situation and let him have his shot. He was out there with me for a few weeks, on a kind of on-going trial. But the club then decided they weren't going to offer him a contract, and told me we were decamping to Turkmenistan or somewhere for a two-week tournament. What the fuck? I threw my toys out of the pram and threatened to go home again. Obviously getting bored of my shenanigans, this time the club were like, 'No, listen, you can't keep doing this. You're under contract. You've already been home once, and the season's only just started!'

The club must have seen how serious I was because the next thing I know they started waving all this money around. They promised to make me the highest paid player at the club, just as long as I agreed to go home only once more during the season. But by then my mind was made up and the next day my brother and I were both on a flight back to London. I went back to Klaipėda after a while, but I kept going back and forth all season. I'd play a couple of games, shoot off to London, go back, play another few games. I must have been a nightmare for the club to deal with. I was still talking to my agent/manager Gary, but losing faith in him fast. On one of my trips back home, I bumped into John Fashanu (Millwall, Wimbledon and England), and he asked if he could become my new agent. Eager for a fresh start, I agreed.

Come that November, which marked the end of the Lithuanian season, I went back to London. I still had another year left on my contract at this point. I had a meeting with Fash in the February or March, and not knowing that was what we did, he was like, 'What? The club haven't paid you since November? That means they're in breach of contract. You're out of it.' So Fash emailed the club to tell them the score, and there was a bit of back and forth between them. I'm not sure what was said, but that was that for me. I never went back to Lithuania and I never spoke to anyone from the club again.

4 MAKING MOVES

Barry Town (2002–03)
Boston United (2003)
Leyton Orient (2003)
Rushden & Diamonds (2003–04)
Doncaster Rovers (2004)
Torquay United (2004–05)

As luck would have it, my leaving FK Atlantas roughly coincided with John Fashanu becoming the new chairman of Barry Town in the League of Wales. They'd traditionally been the dominant force in the Principality, and were coming off the back of a couple of league and cup doubles. They were the first professional club in the country, and played the likes of Dinamo Kyiv, Boavista and Porto in European competitions. Amazingly, they'd even beaten the Portuguese giants 3-1 at Jenner Park, their then home ground. They lost the away leg 8-0 but still, not many teams can say they beat Porto! Fash felt he had all the tools necessary, in particular the money and the contacts, to take the club to the next level and turn them into a bona fide European superpower.

They were interesting times for everyone involved at the South Wales club. Kenny Brown was the manager, and he was a cool guy. Fash was using his influence to get some top-quality players into the club, including a few Nigerian internationals, and he even set up meetings with the Nigeria manager to try and get me in the national side. Even though I was born in England, I qualified because of my mum and dad. I went back to watch a game at Watford, only this time I was in one of the boxes. I walked in, wearing three thick chains like I did at the time, and someone asked me to take them off. I did as they wanted just to keep the peace, but I remember being pissed off about it and thinking, 'I am what I am.' When they had me at the club they didn't appreciate me, and here they are years later still trying to push me around!

The minute I knew I'd be staying in the UK for a while, me

and my older brother put in £1,500 each to buy a Fiat Punto and used it between us. I ended up signing for Barry Town at the back end of the 2001–02 season, then signed up for the next as well. I loved my time there. It was driving distance from London, so I could just jump in the car and be home in-between games if I wanted. The club put me up in nice digs in a nice area, and I still had very few outgoings. I was content. And for that level, they were a useful team. We won the Welsh league and cup double again the season I joined, which was the club's third double in a row. To be that dominant is practically unprecedented. This meant that at the start of my first full season we were playing in the Champions League qualifying stages. This was my third consecutive year playing in Europe. We lost 4-2 on aggregate to FK Vardar from Macedonia, but gave a decent account of ourselves. Life was good. I was hitting the back of the net, too. I averaged over a goal every other game for Barry Town, and for the first time in my career, I was making a bit of money so I was soon able to upgrade from the Fiat Punto to a nice Renault Mégane convertible. There weren't many of those in that part of South Wales at the time, probably still aren't, so I drove around like a boss. You could hear that car coming a mile off.

But then things started to go wrong. The first sign was when the players stopped getting paid. We signed a new goalie, who turned out to be a bit of a loose cannon. He supposedly marched into the office one day and said, 'Look, I don't know what the fuck you're doing with this club, but you brought me here under false pretences and you'd better release me from my contract right now.' And they did. That really set alarm bells ringing. I saw him do that and I was like, 'That's how I need to be!' Not long after, the club went into administration and we all got handed free transfers. The club was forced to recruit players from five or six levels beneath them and went from competing against the giants of Europe to losing 8-0 to Caernarfon Town. It was sad to see, but these things happen in football with alarming regularity. All I could do was try to look after myself and move on.

• • •

As you can probably imagine, the Barry Town fiasco set my career back a few steps. I'd gone from representing clubs in major European tournaments to being unemployed. I started doing trials again, and ended up signing a short-term deal for Boston United in October 2003. I remember getting off the train, and finding myself in the middle of fucking nowhere. I had a word with the manager and he told me to just turn up for games, and not worry about training because I lived so far away. Boston played in the Nationwide League Division Three, as it was called then, so they were a professional club. They had a few good players, including David Noble (Exeter City, Rotherham United) on loan from West Ham the season I was there. On my debut we played Swindon Town in the LDV Vans Trophy and I scored a last-minute winner. We had some good results, and the club wanted me to sign a longer deal. But then Leyton Orient came in for me.

At the time Orient had Lee Thorpe (Bristol Rovers, Torquay United, Swansea City), Jabo Ibehre (MK Dons, Colchester United) and Gary Alexander (Hull City, Millwall) on their books, which was some serious firepower for the Nationwide League Division Three, but one of them got injured and I was brought in on a short-term deal to provide some cover. The best thing about going there was the fact that it was right on my doorstep. I could finish training at 1 p.m. and be home within a few minutes. But even with their injury problems, I didn't get a look in. I played half a game all the time I was there. When the last game of my contract rolled around, the manager, Martin Ling, made me sit in the stand. To this day, I have no idea why I didn't get more game time. It wasn't a fitness issue. We did a beep test when I arrived, and I swear down it was the highest score I've had at any club before or since. It was something ridiculous like 16. I knew I had to impress, so I was just telling myself to go as hard as I could. Anyway, for whatever reason, it wasn't to be. I say I never hold grudges, but I can't help it in that situation because the club signed me, and didn't give me a chance to show what I could do. Ironically enough, even Boston finished above Orient in the league that season, which suggested that the problems there ran deep.

When Martin Ling released me from Orient he told me to ring Brian Talbot, who was then managing Rushden & Diamonds in the Nationwide League Division Two, because I'd played a reserve game against them and absolutely smashed them to bits. So I called him, and he told me to come down and have a word. Rushden & Diamonds were another strong team. Onandi Lowe, the Jamaican international, was there at the time. He was probably one of the best ballers I'd ever trained with. They also had Rodney Jack (Crewe Alex, Torquay United) and Paul Kitson (Newcastle United, West Ham United, Derby County) vying for places up front. Lowe was coming to the end of his career then, but he had the best movement I'd ever seen. His timing was impeccable. You could put two defenders on him, and he would just spin off and make space for himself.

What happened at Rushden & Diamonds was mad, and never happened to me anywhere else. I went down for a trial on the Monday, and I was on the bench for the first team on the Saturday. They'd had Trevor Benjamin (Cambridge United, Coventry City) in on loan from Leicester City and sent him back that week, so a space opened up in the squad. Again, though, I didn't get on the pitch. Not that week or any other; in fact, I didn't make a single appearance for the club in all the time I was there, which was about three months. At one away game, our striker got injured, and Brian Talbot rearranged the whole team rather than put me on striker-for-striker. Brian Talbot was a mouthy guy. Once, he said to me, 'I thought you were big, but you aren't so big. It's the clothes you wear. You wear baggy clothes. That's what makes you look big.'

One Monday morning, he pulled me into the office and told me that despite the fact that I'd trained well and been a model pro for the club, he was letting me go. Because I'd been there a while, I was getting on with a lot of the senior players, and a couple of them even took me under their wings. That was probably the first time I can remember being embarrassed to be let go. I didn't even know what I was doing wrong. At the time, it just seemed like nobody wanted to give me a fair run.

• • •

A guy called Vince who was an associate of mine was helping do my deals at the time, and I remember being in an Internet café in Walthamstow and him telling me that Doncaster Rovers were interested. I didn't know much about them so I Googled them, and saw that they were pushing for automatic promotion from the Nationwide League Division Three. They offered to pay me decent money but I said, 'Nah, tell them I want a bit more.' I couldn't see them quibbling over a little extra. So Vince came back and said he'd asked for more and they took the deal off the table. So then I was like, 'Quick! Ring them back and tell them I'll take the original offer!'

That Doncaster team was fucking powerful. Leo Fortune-West (Gillingham, Rotherham United, Cardiff City) was ahead of me, a big experienced striker, and his was the position I had my eye on. David Penney was the manager, and I got on really well with his assistant. I signed until the end of the season, but still lived in London. I would get the train up most days. It was easier than driving. But I was still doing bits and pieces at St Mary's, and there were days when I wouldn't go into training. I just couldn't be arsed. I would stay up with Mich instead, and I probably missed every other Thursday's training the whole time I was there. Even so, it didn't take me long to form a formidable partnership with Gregg Blundell (Doncaster Rovers, Chester City). We just had great chemistry and worked well together. Behind us we had Paul Green (Derby County, Leeds United and Republic of Ireland) who chipped in with a few goals and more than a few killer passes, and at the back were Steve

Foster (Bristol Rovers, Darlington) and Mark Albrighton (Cambridge United, Stevenage Borough). The team was strong right the way through. I scored four times in nine league games, and we got promoted with three games left and went on to win the league. We had an open-top bus parade through the streets of Doncaster, and there must have been 10,000 people there to see us. I remember the crowd singing at me, 'Bayo, Bayo, give us a dance! Bayo, give us a dance!' I was wearing a suit, so I gave them a wave instead. But the gaffer was like, 'Come on, you know the score. You have to give them what they ask for.' So I broke into my heel-and-toe goal celebration routine, the heel-and-toe being a traditional Jamaican dance.

At the end of the season, David Penney had all the players in for individual meetings. I went in thinking I'd smashed it. I'd scored a few goals, become an instant fans' favourite, and we'd won the league. I'd also done that silly dance in front of loads of people, which I thought must have scored me some brownie points. What more could I have done? So I met with the manager and he goes, 'Yeah, we've decided not to offer you a contract. We'll give you a chance to earn one, but you'll have to come in early next season, and you can't miss a single day's training.'

I was in shock. Completely baffled. Above everything else, I was hurt. I'd put a shift in at Doncaster, and done things for the club. I'd done my job and scored goals there. I thought I deserved better treatment than that. So I just said, 'Nah, you're all right,' and walked out. Afterwards, the assistant manager called me and said Penney was a young manager, and the club as a whole wanted me to sign. Penney was just making a point. I told him I wanted to sign, too. I really did. I was ready to commit, and tie my colours to the mast. But I wasn't going to come back for what was essentially another trial after all I'd done for the club. No way. I'd already proved myself. So the assistant said to leave it with him and he'd talk to Penney on my behalf.

That summer, Torquay United came in for me and offered me the terms I wanted, plus a large bonus if I scored ten goals. For me, that was the clincher. It would give me an achievable target. Something to strive for with a prize at the end. But then, Doncaster threw a spanner in the works by calling me back and saying they would match Torquay's terms. Given the choice, I wanted to stay with Donny. I knew the players, the fans liked me, and the club was buzzing after promotion. And Torquay was a long way from London.

So I went to training at Donny on the Monday, and Penney asked me to take Michelle up with me. After training the next day we were both sitting there and the gaffer asked me if I would be moving up, then asked Mich if she'd be coming up with me. He must have twigged that she was the reason I'd missed so much training the season before. We said yes, as we'd already agreed between us to get a place in Doncaster. We didn't discuss the money at first, because they just said they'd match Torquay's offer. But then it transpired that the deal with Donny was on reduced terms until I actually relocated. After I bought a house in the area, my salary would go up. That was an issue because until I started getting my full salary, I wouldn't be able to afford to move. It was Catch-22. So Mich and I just packed up and left. Torquay was calling.

On the Thursday I went down to Torquay with one of my close friends, who was acting as my representative, and had a sit-down with Leroy Rosenior. He was my first black manager. I liked the things he was saying. He used to be a striker himself for Fulham, QPR and West Ham, and he was telling me he knew how to get the best out of me. There were things he told me that will stay with me for ever. One was to get a photo of what I aspired to have, whether it be a house or a car or whatever, put it up where I could see it every day, and let it be my driving force. Well, at the time I really wanted a BMW X5, so I did what he suggested, got a picture of one, and put it up. The club had just been promoted from League Two to League One, and sold their main goalscorer David Graham (Rangers, Sheffield Wednesday) to Wigan Athletic to raise funds. To take the pressure off, Rosenior told me I wasn't there to replace Graham because we were totally different players. They still had Martin Gritton (Plymouth Argyle, Grimsby Town) at the club, but he wasn't scoring enough and they needed another, more direct option.

We had a little clique of London players there, with me, Zema Abbey (Norwich City, Cambridge United), Leon Constantine (Southend United, Port Vale, York City) and a couple of others including Jo Kuffour, one of my closest friends to this day, and every week we would travel back up to London together. You get that at clubs. There are usually a couple of Londoners in the changing room, and we stick together, as do northern lads or guys from anywhere else in the country. Now, I suppose players from different countries all hang out together rather than different parts of Britain. It's a cultural thing. Every club I've been at, I try to be inclusive. I go around before training and shake everyone's hand. The interesting thing about that is when people see me doing it, it encourages them to do it as well and we all end up being more harmonious.

Wherever they are in the world, London people hang with London people. For some reason, though, I sensed a bit of resentment from Rosenior because of it. If he came into the canteen and saw five black guys at the same table he'd make comments about it like, 'Ah, look at the brothers all sitting together.' The players weren't even thinking in those terms. It just made sense for the guys from the same place to sit together because we had more things in common and more to talk about. It was made even weirder by the fact that Rosenior was a London lad himself.

As it happened, his ideal car was an X5 too, and he bought one. A nice 3.0 litre silver number. He drove it to training, not knowing that mine was coming the very next day. Except mine was a 4.4 litre, and it had TVs built into the headrests. That's when I noticed the resentment go up a few notches. He had a lot of racial issues early in his career, and would say things like, 'You lot don't know how hard us older black players had it.' But actually, I did know, because two years earlier I'd been getting the same thing out in Lithuania. I felt he couldn't accept how much things had moved on in the footballing world and how much the landscape had changed. These days, if someone racially abuses a player they can find themselves on the end of criminal charges. But when he was playing, it was part of the game.

Something similar happened to Zema Abbey, who had a Lincoln Aviator customised and flown in. We were training one morning, and we saw it being driven across the training ground. But Zema was training with us, which obviously meant someone else was driving his car. When we looked, it was the gaffer, and he still had his boots on. It felt as if he didn't think we'd worked hard enough to have this kind of money and these luxurious cars.

Where it all came to a head is when the gaffer benched me. I don't think it was anything personal. I wasn't mature enough to see it at the time, but I know I can be inconsistent. It's probably the same with most players. You can't be on it all the time. It just doesn't work that way. So during one of those bad patches, he dropped me. I was playing so badly that at one point, he sent me on for the last fifteen minutes of a game, and almost subbed me off again. We played an away match and lost, and he still didn't bring me on. So I walked back to the changing room, moaning to myself about not getting on when the team needed a goal, and started taking my boots off.

As every footballer knows, if you don't play in the game, you have to do running back out on the pitch after the game. I was frustrated because we'd lost. I didn't want to go out running, but I was prepared to do it. Then, as the gaffer was talking to the team, he pointed at me and declared I had a bad attitude. I was like, 'What? You want me to be happy that I didn't get any game time?' So he walks away mumbling to himself, and I said, 'Why are you mumbling? You're supposed to be the boss. If you have something to say, come out with it.' He turned around to walk back at me in what I perceived to be an aggressive manner. For me, by this point it had stopped being about player to manager and started being about man to man, and I was ready to put him to sleep. Kevin Dearden (Brentford,

Wrexham), our goalkeeper, who also did a bit of coaching, got in between us and managed to get me out of the changing room until I calmed down. I did the running, got on the coach, and after that we didn't talk about the incident again. I suppose I could've got in real trouble, but there were no comebacks. I think everyone knows emotions run high around football, especially when the team puts so much into a match only to lose, and things are often said in the heat of the moment. I don't have any animosity toward Leroy at all. Flash points like that happen in football all the time. There's a lot at stake, and that pressure has to come out somehow.

Torquay was a lovely place, especially in the summer. That part of the world is beautiful. But it was a very up-and-down season for the club. I had a quiet start, but scored a few goals after Christmas and ended up top scorer that season with 14 goals in 37 league games. I scored past Doncaster in both games, which was satisfying. It was my way of sticking my middle finger up to the manager and letting him know he'd made a mistake in letting me go. We'd struggled all season, but finished strong and gave ourselves a chance of staying up with four straight wins over MK Dons, Port Vale, Oldham and Blackpool. But in the end, it wasn't quite enough to stop us being relegated on 51 points after a 2-1 defeat at Colchester in the last game of the season. It was the same total as MK Dons, who stayed up on goal difference. That was how close we came. Torquay fans still hit me up now, and tell me how much they loved me playing there.

Midway through the season, Martin Gritton had left for Grimbsy Town. Before he went he told me his agent, Dean Baker, wanted to meet me. Straightaway when I met him, I knew Dean was my guy. We just gelled. A lot of people ask me how I choose my agent. To me, it's simple. Agents are hustlers. They can dress it up all they want, but at the end of the day, they're hustlers. Plain and simple. The agent you choose should be the one that hustles you the best, because if they're that good at hustling you, imagine how good they'll be hustling managers on your behalf when there's a lot of money at stake!

When a club is relegated, it often sparks wholescale changes. Players and staff come and go and there's a lot of restructuring, mainly geared toward consolidating and cost-cutting. During the summer, I had a chat with my new agent, Dean, and he asked me what I wanted to do. I told him I wanted to stay in League One. At the time, Bristol City were showing interest. After that, and because I'd let something slip to a reporter, it came out in the press that I wouldn't be signing for another season at Torquay. But Torquay weren't keen on letting me go. As I was still under the age of twenty-four, they wanted compensation for me. Bristol City didn't want to go to a tribunal, so they made a couple of offers and things were dragging on a bit. Then I got a message on my answerphone saying, 'Hello. It's Kenny Jackett, manager of Swansea City Football Club. Please give me a call back.'

That was the call that changed the course of my career.

5 THE JACK REVOLUTION

Swansea City (2005–07)

When I got that call from Kenny Jackett, Swansea City weren't exactly on my radar. Our paths must never have crossed. I passed the information on to Dean Baker (my agent and loyal friend to this day) and let him work his magic. In my head I was already on my way to Bristol. I'd worked out that it was only two hours or so away from London, much closer than Torquay. I wanted to keep the family in London where they could be settled, while I did the moving around. I didn't have kids at the time, but Mich and I were serious and had started looking for a house, so being closer to London was always going to be a big factor for me. Dean, consummate businessman as he is, thought it would be a good idea to go down and meet the Swansea City representatives just to have a look at the set-up they had down there and see what kind of contract they'd be offering. On the drive down, all I was thinking was that Swansea is further away from London than Bristol. The meeting was at the new Liberty Stadium, which had just been finished in time for the new season. The moment I saw it I was blown away. I was like, 'What? Who the fucking hell are Swansea?' The stadium was massive. I think it was almost the same capacity then as it is now, 20,000-plus.

We sat down with Jackett and the chairman, Huw Jenkins, and then I found out they'd just been promoted to League One. I listened to what they said, then I told them what they wanted to hear. 'I live, breathe, and eat football. Nothing is more important to me. I'm a model pro. I don't go out much and never drink alcohol. But I'm also willing to learn, and adapt my game to suit the club's philosophy.' At some point thereafter, they wanted to talk about money. That's where I passed things over to Dean. I told them a player and a manager should talk about tactics and how to win games, the money side should be handled by a third party. Someone who knew what they were doing.

The club seemed to respect that. I went out for a while, and when Dean came out he told me they were doubling my money up from what I was getting at Torquay, and keeping the £10,000 bonus for ten goals in place. As well as that, he'd negotiated a £500 appearance bonus and a £500 win bonus. I immediately thought, 'What the fuck?' This was a club that meant business. They weren't messing about. And what was more, judging by the money they were putting on the table, they really wanted me. That felt good.

I told Dean that the only thing stopping me signing on the spot was the location. He went back in to see them, probably in a bid to get some more money, and when he came out said that the club had a car school coming from Bristol every day, where a lot of their players were based, and we'd take turns driving. It's common at clubs. We just change the name from car pool to car school. Apart from cutting your expenses and driving time, when you're new at a club, it's the quickest way of getting to know people. Dean then phoned Bristol City and told them I was about to put pen to paper with Swansea, but they were still stalling. So then, in a moment of clarity, I just thought, 'Let's do this!' and signed. We got in the car and drove back to London, and the moment we arrived, Bristol City called back and said, 'We're ready for you to sign now.' Obviously, by then it was too late. I was a Swansea City player.

When I arrived there, one of the first people I saw was Kevin Austin (Leyton Orient, Lincoln City), who'd just signed for the club from Bristol Rovers. When I'd been at Doncaster, me and him had had a proper ding dong, to the extent that we sparked an ugly ten-man brawl on the field and I was throwing people off left and right to try to get at him. We both got sent off that day. Then, suddenly, we were teammates. The moment we saw each other, we both just burst out laughing. I bought a house near his in Bristol not long after. Kevin was a few years older than me, and he not only became my friend, but also my mentor. He's intelligent and a very inspirational guy. When we started getting close, he told me a lot of things that I took to heart and carried with me. We were chatting one day, and he said, 'What a lot of younger players don't realise is that it's not the car you drive when you're playing football that matters, it's the car you're driving when you finish. That's what determines how well you've done.' It was things like that which made me look up to him. He commanded respect, but in a nice way.

For me, signing for Swansea at the age of twenty-three was a big eye-opener. There was the new stadium to consider, the facilities were top-notch, the coaches and staff were all a class above, and then there were the players. I was surrounded by ballers. Good quality, skilful pros. From top to bottom, the club was maintained the way you would hope a football club to be maintained. Personally, I'd been around a bit by then and had my share of kicks in the teeth. It made a pleasant change to be at a big, well-run club.

Three or four weeks in, the gaffer was telling everyone how happy he was with the progress I was making. But to me, they were four of the worst weeks of my whole career. The warm-up at the beginning of one of my first training sessions involved running up sand dunes, and it almost killed me. I never want to do that again. I was the last one in. I'd literally only just arrived, lugging this massive green *Only Fools and Horses* suitcase behind me. The next thing I knew I was running up and down sand dunes. Anyone who thinks that sounds easy obviously hasn't tried it. When I finished I just lay on the floor gasping, trying to get my breath back. For me, the fitness aspect was tough. I kept thinking I was projecting a bad image, when I really needed to be doing the opposite.

I got it into my head that they didn't rate me, and that gave me something to prove. In my mind, the only way to rectify the situation was to show how superior I was in other areas. With me, that's always going to be strength. I got it into my head that during the training session I was going to shoulder-barge someone, hard, and make my presence known that way. So I went out there, zeroed in on my target, and gave him my best shot. Bang! They didn't even budge. The dude just gave me a look. That left me thinking, 'Not only are these boys fitter, faster, and more skilful than me, but most of them are fucking stronger than me, too.' So where did I fit in?

Like I said, I've always been big. But until that point, I'd never actually done any weight-training. All the muscle I had was a natural result of being a footballer. I remember taking legitimate pride in telling people that I didn't lift weights. I didn't need to. I had the body anyway. We sometimes trained at a gym in Glamorgan, which was the same one the Neath Swansea Ospreys rugby team used. One day they were doing arms, so I joined in with them. I was doing pretty well. I was lifting more than they were. At least, I thought I was, until one of their guys came over and said to me, 'Look, you're doing it all wrong. You're using your back. Stand still, don't rock, and just use your biceps.' He stood over me while I did it to make sure my technique was there, and this time I couldn't get the weight up past the halfway point! I remember it like it was yesterday. That was the day I decided I was going to start weight-training. I couldn't allow myself to get dumped on like that again by a rugby player.

As with any club, I had to do an initiation at Swansea. We were in some army barracks – looking around there were loads of soldiers and sailors, as well as the team – having lunch in the canteen when it was decided that the new signings should all sing a song. With my background, it didn't bother me at all. I might not be the best singer in the world, but you can bet I'm better than half of any given football team. I just got on the chair and gave a rendition of either 'Stand by Me' or 'Lean on Me', I can't remember which. I think me just going for it and showing the squad that despite my size I could still have some banter really made them take to me.

Something else that endeared me to my teammates happened in training the next day. We had to ride bikes. Except mine was messed up, and wouldn't go anywhere. Everyone else, including the guy who fixed the bikes when they broke down, went flying way off in front. I didn't know how I was going to catch them, so I picked the bike up, put it over my shoulder, and started running. All the team saw was this big black guy coming over the hill carrying a bike. They all just cracked up laughing. The banter was something new to me. People would be cracking mum jokes and stuff and I'd be sitting there cringing and thinking, 'What're you doing? That's straight fighting talk where I'm from!' Lee Trundle (Wrexham, Bristol City) was the absolute worst for it. Him and Andy Robinson were always playing tricks on each other. Lee even did a poo in Andy's training kit, then folded it up and put it back where he found it!

On the third day I was there the 7/7 bombings took place, and I remember not being able to get hold of some of my people and being mad worried about everything. I had a word with the gaffer and told him I wouldn't be able to concentrate on anything else until I knew everyone was safe, so he said it was okay for me to drive back to London. I remember driving into the city and noticing how eerily quiet it was. A lot of things changed after that day. It hit the country right where it hurts. If you can take any positives from something like that, it's a reminder of how fragile and precious life is. We all get so wrapped up in our jobs and whatever else, we sometimes forget the important things.

When I first went to Swansea, I didn't speak much. Back in those days, I didn't want to get involved too much in changing-room politics and all the rest of it. I didn't want the distractions. I just wanted to get on with what I had to do. I doubt any manager would ever say I was a quiet guy, but in team meetings and the like, I just let other people have their say. My attitude was more, 'You work out what you think might be wrong, and then we can fix it.' One thing I knew was that I had a lot of work to do at Swansea, so I put my head down and got the hours in. Six weeks or so later, I was up to speed.

In the first-ever game at the Liberty Stadium, against Tranmere Rovers, I scored the goal in a 1-0 victory. Jackett got us up to such a standard that for the first few months of the season, after we'd lost a couple of games early-doors, we were blowing everyone out of the water. We put seven on Bristol City, five on both Chesterfield and Walsall. Nobody could touch us. I played up front with Lee Trundle. I could see he was gifted straightaway. As well as being another big, strong lad he had a great touch and would do things with a football you didn't think were possible. I learned a lot from him. Not just on-the-pitch stuff, but I loved how he handled people calling him fat and that kind of thing. He would embrace it. And it's true that people don't boo bad players. Opposition supporters only boo you if they see you as a threat. That season, we had Roberto Martínez (Zaragoza, Wigan Athletic), Leon Britton (Swansea City, Sheffield United) and Owain Tudur Jones (Norwich City, Inverness Caledonian Thistle and Wales) in midfield, and at the back were Alan Tate (Royal Antwerp, Leeds United), Sam Ricketts (Hull City, Wolverhampton Wanderers, Bolton Wanderers), captain Garry Monk (Southampton and Barnsley), Kristian O'Leary, a Swans legend, and my mate Kevin Austin, with Willy Guéret (Le Mans, MK Dons, Millwall) between the sticks. That is one hell of a team for League One.

The gaffer then wanted to consolidate things, and in the January transfer window spent a small fortune bringing in Leon Knight (Sheffield Wednesday, MK Dons) from Brighton & Hove Albion where he'd been scoring goals for fun. He also brought in another forward, Rory Fallon (Barnsley, Plymouth Argyle and

My childhood – many happy memories growing up in north London. My smile hasn't changed a bit!

Above: Mum and Dad – the backbone of our family. I'm so blessed to have them in my life. My strong moral compass is down to them.

Right: Looking sharp with my brothers Dele (left) and Yemi (centre). Where I go, they go – we roll as a team.

Above: My wonderful family – the reason I work so hard is for them.

With my children – teaching them that Beast Mode is a way of life!

Above: The legend Stevie G – a good friend and one of my Liverpool idols.
Below: Celebrating with my Play-Off Winner's Medal for AFC Wimbledon and my Players' Player and Fans' Player of the Year awards for Wycombe.

Above: Catching up with some famous faces. Clockwise from top left: Premier League royalty, Thierry Henry and Didier Drogba, top actor Colin Salmon, Southampton supremo Virgil van Dijk, Chelsea maestro Eden Hazard and NFL powerhouse Menelik Watson.

Left: My kids and extended family going full Beast Mode.

Left: I'm big on team celebrations. This was the fake KO celebration after scoring against Grimsby this season. It's good for team spirit to have a bit of fun. Even Dwayne 'The Rock' Johnson tweeted me when I did the 'People's Elbow' celebration.

Right: The agony. My penalty miss against Barnsley in the Play Off Final, 2006. A painful day for me.

Below: The ecstasy. Lifting the Footbal League Trophy after my winner for Swansea against Carlisle at the Millennium Stadium in 2006 alongside fellow goalscorer Lee Trundle and the gaffer, Kenny Jacket.

Above: Arguably one of my proudest – and most surreal – moments in life. Scoring for AFC Wimbledon against Liverpool in the FA Cup. Being a big Liverpool fan, it felt mad, but what a feeling it was. We put a good shift in that day.

Below: A special feeling not only for me but for everyone at AFC Wimbledon. To score and get promoted in front of your own fans at Wembley – does it get any better than that?

One of my greatest days in football. Winning promotion for AFC Wimbledon at Wembley . . .

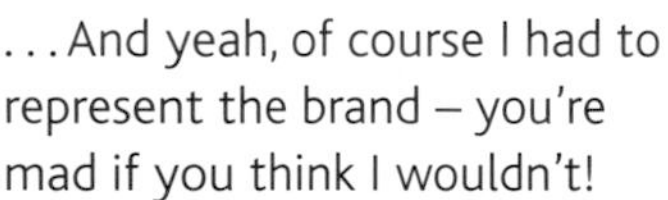

. . . And yeah, of course I had to represent the brand – you're mad if you think I wouldn't!

New Zealand) from Swindon Town, for £300,000. That was a record fee for Swansea at the time. These were players who had to justify the outlay. And there was already competition for the striking positions with me and Lee Trundle.

At clubs, footballers always weigh up who their direct competition is in the starting eleven. Trundle was the golden boy at Swansea so his place in the team was cemented, and Leon Knight was a different kind of player, so I saw Fallon as my main threat. I did go and see the gaffer about it to see where I stood, and it did me no favours whatsoever. I would love Kenny Jackett to manage me now, with me knowing how he is and him knowing how I am, because he is hands-down the most confusing manager I've ever worked with. You'd go in his office to complain about something, and when you came out your head would be in bits. I'd be saying to him, 'Look, I think I'm the best in my position but I'm not getting much playing time.' Jackett would reply, 'Yep, yep, yep, I understand. You're right, B. You are. I get it. Don't worry. Cheers. Thanks for coming to see me. Bye now.'

When I came out the other players would ask what he said, and I'd have to think for a moment then reply, 'I haven't got a fucking clue.'

As much as I despised playing second fiddle to Fallon, he went through the horrors a bit and the pressure got to him.

The fans, who I had a great relationship with, would call for me to come on from the bench and I began seeing the benefits of that. By the time the gaffer put me on, I'd be playing against some real heavy legs, which only made my game easier. I would come on and look amazing. I remember Leon Knight's debut against MK Dons. He scored a hat-trick, and I set up two of the goals. Afterwards, the press started calling us Little and Large. He is still one of the best finishers I've ever played with.

A few weeks after he signed for Swansea, we played up at Port Vale and lost 3-2. On the coach coming home I was talking to Kevin Austin about Mich and I called her 'the wife'. Anyone who knows him will tell you Leon Knight is really mouthy. He's about five foot five, and has a wicked case of Little Man Syndrome which gets him into bother sometimes. Suddenly, he turned around, butted into the conversation, and said to me, 'Bruv, you're not married.'

I tried to brush it off and just said, 'No, but that's what I call her. You know what I mean.' Then I went back to Kevin and continued our talk, when Knighty piped up again. 'Oi, bruv, you're not married. So stop saying she's your wife, innit?'

So then I stood up on the coach and said, 'Look, Knighty, real talk, check yourself.'

The gaffer was on a different coach, thank God, but Kevin Austin, who'd somehow got himself in between us, and Garry

Monk had to hold me back. Kevin Nugent got involved, too. He was a quiet man, Kevin, but he had respect, and when he put his foot down you knew when to ease up. I wouldn't say any of us were scared of him, but we all knew he could fight. He came up the bus and told Knighty to reel it in. That only made him worse; he started saying, 'Wait a minute, why's everyone coming at me for? I'm telling the truth. He kept calling the woman his wife, *and they ain't fuckin' married*!' and then he looked right at me and went, 'Why are you standing there like you're going to do something? If you're going to do something, *do it*!'

I couldn't hold myself back any more, so I lunged for him. But by this time the whole coach was standing and there were too many bodies in the way. If I'd managed to get hold of him, I swear I would have popped his head like a pimple. We didn't talk for four days, and when we did I told him that if he stepped out of line again or even said the wrong thing, I was going to put him to sleep. Ever since then, we've been tight. He's a London boy, and likes everyone to know it. That day, he must have forgotten that I'm a London boy too.

Not long after, Mich and I did tie the knot. Kind of. With her being half-Nigerian and half-West Indian we had a traditional wedding, but didn't get married in a legal sense. We were having our first child and our parents thought we'd better do something traditional so the people back in their old villages in Nigeria would accept the child. It was basically just a big glorified party, which is what I believe weddings to be anyway. I had to lie down on the floor, and my boys threw money on me until her dad said it was enough. It was a spectacle. Another traditional aspect involved my dad. He was sitting there and three girls came out. The first two would be dressed exactly like Mich, and my dad would have to say, 'No, that's not my daughter.' Eventually, Mich would come out and he'd be able to say, 'There she is.'

• • •

Even after Knighty and Fallon arrived at Swansea, I was always involved in the team. We got to the LDV Vans Trophy (now the EFL Trophy) final at the Millennium Stadium in Cardiff, where we played Carlisle United. Because the new Wembley was still being built, all the play-off and cup finals were played at the Millennium so we went there a couple of times during my time at Swansea. That was my first taste of playing football in front of 45,000 people in the UK. We won 2-1 and I scored the winner off Trundle's flick. It was all soured a bit when after the game Trunds and Alan Tate got arrested on suspicion of public order offences – waving a flag around which had FUCK CARDIFF written on it and wearing T-shirts that showed a guy in a white football shirt pissing on a blue one. This was all to do with Swansea's rivalry with Cardiff City. Everyone knows there are little local rivalries between a lot of clubs, but of all the clubs I'd been at to that point Swansea and Cardiff's was the most intense. As the game moves forward, thankfully the crowd trouble is getting less and less.

We also won the FAW Premier Cup by beating Wrexham 2-1, and just a few weeks after our LDV Vans Trophy victory we were back at the Millennium Stadium for the play-off final against Barnsley. They'd finished fifth in the league, and we'd finished sixth. Nobody scored more goals than us, though. We banged in 78 in the 46 games. But for the final they had me and Trundle, who had scored about 35 goals between us, on the bench and Knighty and Fallon started. To be fair Fallon scored, along with Andy Robinson, to grab a 2-2 draw, and send the game to penalties. I've never called myself a penalty-taker. There's been a designated penalty-taker already in place whenever I've gone anywhere, so I never really got much practice. I was always confident, though. I'd taken one before in a cup tie and slotted it in. I remember putting the ball down and whistling. It was a crucial stage; I was the third taker, and nobody had missed so the score was 2-2 in pens. I struck it, and watched helplessly as the ball went sailing over the bar. Everything fell silent. I remember thinking, 'Oh shit, I missed!' But I still had faith in the footballing gods. I was convinced things would come right, and we'd get promoted because we'd been the better team in the league.

The other penalty-takers all kept on scoring, and it looked like I was going to be the only one, on either side, who'd missed. So then my thought process changed from hoping our keeper saved one, to hoping one of the other Swansea boys missed just so I wouldn't have to live with the stigma. It would have hurt a lot, after a long, gruelling season, to be the only reason we didn't get promoted. I know how selfish that sounds, but I just couldn't be the only one. So then Alan Tate steps up, and he misses as well. I swear, as horrible as this sounds, part of me was relieved that I wouldn't have to carry the burden alone.

I was never an emotional guy when it came to football. It's a game. You take the highs and lows, the good and the bad. Sometimes it drives you mad, and sometimes it takes you to the edge of heaven. But I could never even imagine myself shedding tears on the pitch because of something that happened during a match. But when the shoot-out ended and the Barnsley players and fans were going mental around us, I remember sinking to my knees and thinking, 'Wow, we lost, and it was my fault.' What made me tear-up was when Roberto Martínez came up and hugged me. He was crying. Not just crying, weeping.

Prior to that he'd fallen out with the manager, maybe because of rumours flying around that he was after the gaffer's job, so he wasn't even playing, he was in the dugout in a suit. Seeing how much it meant to him made me emotional. I could see the pain in his eyes, and how much he loved Swansea. It was overwhelming. Looking back, if I had been the player I became as I got older, mentally, I would have handled it easier, and would have taken the miss on the chin.

All this happened on a Saturday. The next morning I was due to fly to Miami to join my brothers on a boys' holiday. I'd booked the flights months before, thinking we would be promoted already and there was no way we'd be playing in the play-offs. Walking out of the ground, I didn't speak to anyone. A reporter asked me for an interview and I just blanked him. I sat slumped in the back of the coach, went home, got changed, and went straight to the airport. My brothers had heard about what happened, so when I arrived at the hotel I just kind of fell into their arms and then we went out and got blitzed. The best thing was there was no coverage of the English play-offs in the media over there so I wasn't reminded of it a million times. So yeah, that first season at Swansea was nothing if not eventful.

Another incident that stands out was the day we were at the gym training when two guys came looking for Izzy Iriekpen (Bristol City, Scunthorpe United), one of our defenders. I think it was some disagreement over a girl. One of the guys was wearing a Cardiff City top, which was never going to go down well in the middle of Swansea. I saw Izzy walking toward these two characters by himself, ready to take them on, so I raced over to back him up just as two cars pulled up. Before the cars even stopped, there were people piling out of them. It was like a TV cop show. One of the guys was about six foot six and wearing a trench coat, and the other one was carrying a hammer. I thought, 'Fuck me, this is going to be a scrap!'

The next thing I hear is one of the guys who got out of the cars shouting, 'Where are the fuckin' Cardiff boys?'

Then I realised they were on our side. Swansea has a good firm, and these were boys who came to watch us play all the time. They knew everything. And somehow it must have got back to them that some Cardiff boys were in Swansea looking to have a go at Izzy. They were there within minutes. When these Swansea lads turned up, the boy in the Cardiff City top ran off, while his mate started saying the reason he was there was nothing to do with football, it was about his girlfriend or whatever. To be fair, the Swansea fans always backed their team, no matter what. In the end, I think it was all sorted out amicably enough. I've never experienced it personally, but there's a soft element attached to a footballer which often makes other people think they can take them on. The public often just assume we are all pampered little boys who never grow up. That wasn't the case with Izzy. He was never the type to take any shit. He always backed himself and would stand up to people no matter what.

Because the guys in the firms are so close to the clubs, you often get to know them socially. They go to every game, all the fundraisers and events. The clubs are the centre of their lives. At Swansea, they were all cool with me. At one open day, I was playing with the kids and chatting to this stocky guy who had his calf strapped up. I thought he might have injured himself having a kickabout, so I asked him and he said, 'Nah. I pulled it stamping on someone's head.' He was so casual about it. His kid was ten feet away!

The next season, there was a general feeling around the club that we'd come so close the last time, we couldn't fail to get promoted this time around. Kenny Jackett was still the manager and we'd managed to keep the squad together, as well as making a couple of shrewd additions. For some reason though, the buzz had gone, and we didn't start very well. We went out of all the cups early-doors and in the February Jackett left by mutual consent. The first game after that happened was Doncaster Rovers away. We didn't win, but Trundle and I both scored in a 2-2 draw. Next up was a midweek game against Scunthorpe United at the Liberty on 20 February 2007. I didn't feel well before the game, so I rang my mum and asked her to say a prayer for me, but I still wanted to play. That Scunthorpe team were decent. It was 0-0 coming up to the 43rd minute and I went up to chest the ball. As I did so, my studs stuck in the turf and I got tangled up with Steve Foster, who I was with at Doncaster, and the weight of both of us came down on my right leg. I don't remember hearing or feeling a pop or a crack like you hear other people tell it. I just remember a searing pain, then grabbing the back of my calf and thinking, 'That shit hurts!'

I knew I couldn't continue, so I sat back down on the turf and waited for a stretcher. When it came, one side couldn't hold my weight and they dropped me. It must have looked comical from the stands because I remember the crowd all going 'Hooray!' The fans didn't know how bad the injury was.

I could tell by the amount of pain I was in that I'd never had an injury like it before, but I realised how serious it was when I was in the changing room at half-time getting gas and air and Steve Foster and Scunthorpe's other centre-half came in to apologise and wish me well. Then the ambulance came and took me to the hospital. While I was waiting for X-rays, a doctor told me that if it wasn't broken I'd be out for six weeks, but if it was broken I'd be out for six months or more. That gave me a bit of hope, but that was dashed when a surgeon came in and after one look said it was definitely broken, and I'd be going in for surgery the next day. It was surreal. I went to the hospital with Kevin Austin, so I asked him to call my brother Yemi and let the family know. Yemi said the moment he answered the phone, he knew something was up. The family came up the next day, just before my operation. Mich was pregnant at the time and on holiday in Grenada, so I told them not to tell her. I didn't want her to be stressed. It wasn't like she could do anything.

When I woke up the next day, the doctors told me that during the op I'd had compartment syndrome, which is caused by excessive swelling or bleeding within an enclosed bundle of muscles, so they had to cut me and leave the wound open to alleviate the pressure. They explained it was so serious that if they'd stitched me up with compartment syndrome, I might have lost my leg, which as you can probably imagine wouldn't be at all good for a professional footballer. As a result of the compartment syndrome, a few days after the initial op I had a skin graft. I was in the hospital for eight or nine days altogether. The most humbling thing was that while I was there, every single player came to see me independently at different times. The whole squad. I've been at clubs where other players have broken their legs, and I didn't go to see them. Lee Trundle was going out with Liz McClarnon out of Atomic Kitten at the time and one day he brought her along to see me. Garry Monk brought me pizza. Not quite the same thing as bringing a girl band member, but I was very appreciative of both. Around this time, Roberto Martínez was given the manager's job, and he also came to see me and said he wanted me to stay for the next season. I said that was fine by me, I had unfinished business. I'd had some great times at Swansea, and I didn't want the fans' last memories of me to be seeing me get carried off the field on a stretcher.

Because I'd been in bed for nine days dosed up on morphine, getting mobile again was hard work. Morphine kills your appetite. You just don't want to eat. I lost a lot of weight. I was walking through Walthamstow on crutches with my younger brother, and no less than four different people that we knew from back in the day stopped us and told me how small I looked. My brother still laughs about it today, but I hated the feeling. I was probably the smallest I'd been since I was a kid. I think I was about 94 kilos. So two days after I was discharged I was riding a bike again. I hadn't eaten properly or worked out for all that time, and I just couldn't stand it any more. The season hadn't yet finished, so I threw myself into rehab trying to get back playing as soon as possible.

I had a chat to Dean, my agent, and he contacted the club about extending my contract. When he got back to me he said the offer was another year on the same terms. That was a slap in the face. Firstly, the club were saying that I hadn't improved as a player in two years, and, secondly, I broke my leg playing for them. I thought I deserved a better deal. So I sent Dean back to Huw Jenkins with a counter-offer. I would stay on the same money until I finished my recuperation, and when I played my first game back I wanted a 25 per cent rise. The club refused. That made me feel undervalued and underappreciated. I knew Gillingham were interested in me because they'd made enquiries in the January transfer window when Kenny Jackett was still there and he'd knocked them back. So Dean tested the water and it turned out they still wanted me. Furthermore, they were willing to offer me almost twice what I was getting at Swansea. I'd never been on that money before so that made the decision easy. Swansea gave me a deadline to decide. My parents wanted me to sign there, and maybe Dean did too, but when the time came I just couldn't do it. My head had been turned.

As the old saying goes, hindsight is a beautiful thing, and, in the years since, I've questioned my decision to leave Swansea many times. My two years there were an education and set me up for everything else that was to come, in every conceivable way. It was the first club I really fell in love with, and everything was a higher standard than what I'd seen previously. I learned how successful clubs operate, and on a practical level I managed to buy houses in Bristol and London, so in that sense I was able to safeguard my future a little bit. That season, the club missed out on the play-offs, but Martínez stabilised them and they would be in the Premier League a couple of seasons later. Martínez has moved on, but the club have been there ever since. Looking back, I'm pretty sure that if I hadn't broken my leg, I too would have got to the Premier League, either with Swansea or with someone else. But there's no point in being bitter. You can't help but be philosophical about situations like that and think that maybe everything happens for a reason.

6 BACK TO THE DRAWING BOARD

Yeovil Town (2007)
Millwall (2007)
Northampton Town (2008–10)

Instead of re-signing for Swansea, I went and had a meeting at Gillingham with chairman Paul Scally and manager Ronnie Jepson instead. By this time, it was the end of May or beginning of June. Gillingham asked if I'd be playing again by pre-season. I told them I'd just come off crutches, and was still three or four months away from full fitness. That put me on course for a September return. They said they'd been under the impression that it was a six-month injury lay-off, which would have meant I'd be back by July. I told them I'd love to be back playing that soon, but the way the recovery was going, it wasn't going to be possible. It hadn't been a straightforward break, if such a thing exists. I'd had to wait for the skin graft to heal and X, Y and Z. Ronnie Jepson said, 'Well, if I get off to a bad start I'm going to get sacked, and I can't afford to be signing players I won't be able to use until a quarter of the season is over.'

Eventually, they said they'd pay me expenses and let me do the rest of my rehab at Gillingham. Then, as soon as I was fully fit again, I could sign. That wasn't going to work for me. I had outgoings and responsibilities. I needed to be taking home a pay packet. Around that time, Swindon Town started showing an interest in me. Their manager, Paul Sturrock, got in touch and told me he wanted to set up a meeting. I went down there for a medical and failed it, because I still wasn't fit. By now, time was marching on and the new season was starting, but I still didn't have a club. I asked Dean what was going on, and he didn't have any answers. In retrospect, it's clear that any interested parties were waiting to see what I would be like when my leg healed. A lot of players don't come back from injuries like that. Plus, nobody wants to be paying a sizeable percentage of their salary budget to someone who wasn't even able to play.

In July I got my last payment from Swansea, and the following month Mich and I had our first child. Thankfully, the birth went incredibly smoothly. We left the house when Mich went into labour at around six o'clock, got checked into the hospital at eight, and were discharged by twelve with a new addition to our family, a beautiful baby girl we called Kamira. Obviously, the timing wasn't ideal. I had no income, we had two cars, and I was paying the mortgages on two houses. Added to all that, during all the tests and treatment I was having I discovered that my right leg was fractionally shorter than my left. It might have been caused by the break, or it might have been like that all along. I'm not sure. The first couple of months we used our savings, then I had to take out a couple of loans and there were still no clubs interested. I remember thinking, 'Wow, shit got real.'

One positive thing about being injured and out of the game for so long was the fact that it gave me a lot of time to spend with Kamira. For the first three months, we were together almost all the time. That meant we had an amazing bond, and still do. Probably the only other positive is that it gives me the opportunity to wind people up. If I'm on the beach or something and people see my scar, it's so noticeable that they almost always comment on it. Over the years I've developed a range of stories, my favourite being the one where I tell people, in glorious detail, about the time I got bitten by a shark in the Dominican Republic while I was saving some kids. People fall for it every single time.

Not being able to play football also meant that I had more time and energy to devote to my gym work and weight-training. Until then, I'd been doing it slowly and making steady progress, but wasn't into it religiously. When I first came out of hospital I could have maintained the same weight and my new streamline build, but I just felt like that wasn't me. The rehab was going well, but I was aware of the fact that I'd never be as fast as I used to be and that I had to change the way I played. The doctors told me that after a bad break the average player loses around 10 per cent of his athleticism. No matter how hard you work, you will only ever be about 90 per cent of the player you were before the injury.

I made a conscious decision to focus more on my upper-body strength, and adapt my game accordingly. I knew I had to maintain a balance. If I wasn't a footballer I'd have spent more time lifting weights and got a lot bigger a lot faster. But I tried to keep a lid on it because I knew I had to run around, and the more weight you're carrying, the harder that is. Even so, it's probably fair to say I got addicted to the weight work. We all have addictions and vices, and the gym turned into mine. When people saw me working out, unless they knew who I was, they often assumed I was a weightlifter training for a competition. To this day, I have to reel myself in and make sure I do forty minutes of cardio before I hit the weights, even if I go after a game. It's not even a chore to do it that way. I like a rounded work-out. I can do my time on the running or rowing machine then say to myself, 'Right, that's in the bank. Now you can go and throw some steel around!'

I was doing rehab and training at Gillingham, but probably because I wasn't affiliated with them the physio didn't pay much attention to me. He just had me running around in circles. Literally. I went up to Lilleshall to get some specialist treatment a couple of times, which was intense. This was when sports science was just coming into its own. It just made it clear to me that I'd probably be better off if I severed my ties with Gillingham. I spoke with Russell Slade, who was manager at Yeovil Town, who'd reached the League One play-offs the season before. He said I could go and do some rehab down there, and when I was fit again they'd sign me. So I began pushing myself and training harder, just so I could get a contract and start earning again. I eventually managed to get back on the pitch in October, nine months after the injury happened and four months after my last pay packet. Weirdly enough, that game was against Swansea City. For the first two minutes I was okay, but after that I just hobbled around and the rest of the game passed me by. They beat us 2-1. That year, Swansea won the league at a canter. Nobody could get near them.

After the game, I got hold of my agent, Dean, and told him to tell Russell Slade I was ready to sign for Yeovil. The gaffer said they'd talk about it tomorrow. That turned out to be the very day Kenny Jackett got the Millwall job, so the first thing he did was ring me up and ask if I was available. I reminded him that I hadn't played for the best part of a year and was barely match-fit. He said it didn't matter. He needed a striker he could trust. The thing was, Russell Slade and Yeovil had been good to me. They'd had my back for the past couple of months and footed the bill for me to go through rehab. I was grateful for that. So I called Slade up, told him Millwall had offered me something, and that I couldn't afford to turn it down. But I told him that because I owed him, if he put a contract in front of me I would sign it. He said we couldn't do it right then, it would take a couple of days to get the paperwork together and iron out all the creases. I couldn't wait around any longer, so I signed for Millwall.

Being a London club, it would have been hard to turn Millwall down anyway. They were also in League One, so it wouldn't mean dropping down a division. I wanted to make a big impact at Millwall. They got me on a three-month contract, and put me straight into the squad for the next game. I reminded Kenny that I wasn't exactly in top physical condition, and that it might take me some time to get my fitness and match sharpness back. Kenny insisted that he just needed a striker. To this day, I still maintain that mainly because I was coming back from a long lay-off, Millwall is probably the only place where I didn't show the fans what I could do. People still say to me, 'I remember you at Millwall. We called you "The Fridge".' And that was because of me looking like the NFL player, William 'The Fridge' Perry, because I was so cool of course. Nevertheless, the fans at the New Den still took to me.

There are two things I'll always be thankful to Kenny Jackett for. One is he came along when he did and got me out of a hole, and the other is he got me fit. Not to put too fine a point on it, by this time, I knew I was playing for my future in the game. That takes its toll mentally, which you have to deal with on top of not being in peak physical condition. I remember a game when I had a couple of weeks left to run on my contract, and I was on the bench. Kenny sent me on with two minutes left just so I could collect my appearance bonus. By the time I got stripped and ran on, there was enough time for me to take a throw-in and the whistle went. I walked off thinking that was the easiest money I'd ever made!

Just as I was getting back to full fitness, Kenny let me know he wouldn't be extending my contract, and I would be a free agent again by the January window. I can't even knock that. I wasn't performing at Millwall. I'd only played a handful of games, and I didn't get on the score sheet once. That's what you have to do when you're a striker. Score goals. It's your job. If you don't do it consistently, questions will be asked. By then, there was a bit of competition up front with me, Lewis Grabban (Rotherham United, Norwich City, Bournemouth), Neil Harris (Nottingham Forest, Southend United), Jason Price (Swansea City, Hull City, Tranmere Rovers) and Will Hoskins (Watford, Bristol Rovers) all at the club. Even so, the team wasn't playing well and I wasn't really justifying my wage. I knew I had to move on.

I had another chat with Dean, and he said there wasn't much around. There were only two clubs showing any interest in my services at all, and they were Northampton and Cheltenham. I didn't know much about either, apart from the fact that Cheltenham Town were a club I always scored against. I just remember thinking even though they were both in League One, they were small clubs. Smaller than Swansea and Millwall, anyway. Whatever I decided, I felt I'd be taking a step backwards. To be honest, at that stage it was probably just what my career needed. There wasn't much to choose between the two, so I just went for the one closest to London, which happened to be Northampton Town.

Being a smaller club, Northampton couldn't offer much money. I wouldn't say it was the bare minimum, but it was close. It was just enough to cover my outgoings and ensure I didn't accumulate any more debt. Now I was back to fitness, I was simply looking for a place I could get my head down and rebuild my reputation. I remember the first day of training, on this big, muddy, rainswept rugby field. We did a circuit, and I came in dead last. I remember thinking to myself, 'What have I done? How did I end up here?' At the same time, I caught sight of Stuart Gray, the Northampton manager, and the look on his face suggested he must have been thinking, 'Who the fuck have I signed?'

But it's funny how things turn out. Going to Northampton Town turned out to be one of the best footballing decisions I ever made. Millwall finished seventeenth in the league that season, and Northampton finished ninth, within striking distance of the play-offs. We played Millwall and beat them. I scored six goals in six games, and finished the season with something like eight goals to my name in barely a quarter of the season. As footballers progress through their careers, the way they play often changes. After I scored the six in six, my mindset shifted. I went from being a straight target-man to being more of a goalscorer. I knew I had the skill and the technique. I always had. But because of my size, most clubs drilled it out of me and just wanted to utilise my strength and presence in the air. Another factor was that after the broken leg I'd lost a bit of pace, so I'd been forced to adapt my game. I was never blessed with electrifying pace to begin with, but I was definitely a yard slower post-injury. I had to evolve.

When Stuart Gray signed me he didn't play me straightaway, so when I finally broke into the team I had a point to prove. When I started banging the goals in, the gaffer told me I didn't have to train, because after so long out I was struggling a bit. He told me to keep on doing what I was doing and get myself ready for the games. We had a good, young team: Giles Coke (Mansfield Town, Motherwell, Sheffield Wednesday), Chris Doig (Nottingham Forest, York City), Mark Bunn (Norwich City, Aston Villa) and Ryan Gilligan (Torquay United, Östersunds) with Mark Little and Daniel Jones on loan from Wolves, and we finished strong.

At the end of the season, Leyton Orient came in for me and offered me a two-year deal. That prompted Northampton to put another offer on the table, and I took it. Under normal circumstances, I would have gone home to London. The only thing stopping me was the fact that Martin Ling was the manager. I'd played under him at Orient before, and didn't get a look-in. I still resented him a bit for that, and I definitely didn't want a repeat. The contracts were exactly the same, the difference was that Northampton weren't paying agent's fees, but Orient were. That meant I had to pay Dean his fee out of my own pocket, and I chose to do it that way. It proved to be the correct decision.

• • •

As smooth and hassle-free as Kamira's arrival into the world was, our second child, Jai, came with bad intentions right from the start. He was meant to come on the eleventh and I was due back from holiday in Miami on the second or third, which would have given us plenty of time to prepare everything. Mich knows how important my holidays are. At the end of a gruelling eight- or nine-month season, it means everything for me to get away for a week or two, and this was especially true earlier in my career.

I used to plan my holidays with military precision. I can be very stubborn about my needs. Some would even say selfish. But nobody knows what I need like I do. It had been a tough year, and I was getting ready to go again. I just needed a break. So there I was with three days left in Miami with my teammate Giles Coke, when Mich called me and said she was going into labour early. What made it even worse was that there was a banging party going on in the background making noise. I agreed to change my flights and get the earliest possible one back. But the thing was, that wouldn't get me back in London until the

Thursday. Then I realised I was probably going to miss the birth. I felt awful. Here I was over the other side of the world. It really put things into perspective.

Of all my children, this turned out to be the worst delivery. During the birth, Mich had what they call a placenta abruption, which is where the placenta separates from the uterus before the baby is born. Blood was gushing out of her. She almost miscarried several times, and when he finally emerged, Jai came out face-down and backwards. I felt so bad about it. I know I should have been there, on that day of all days, and it's something I regret to this day. It was a big wake-up call, and made me realise that it shouldn't be about me all the time. Mich needed me, my family needed me, and I wasn't there. Her mum and my mum both were, which was another reason I couldn't have strolled in the delivery room late. My mum would've whupped my arse. She was firmly in Mich's corner. As was Jai, because I swear to God for the first month of his life he hated me with a passion. He wouldn't even let me pick him up. It was almost as if he knew I'd fucked up and wanted to punish me. After that he began to relax a bit, probably because he thought he'd made me suffer enough.

In my second season at Northampton, they signed Leon Constantine (Brentford, Port Vale, Southend United) from Leeds. I'd played with him at Torquay, so we were able to link up again.

I was the man for them. I used to stay with Giles Coke, and I remember telling him the night before the first game of the season that I was never a natural penalty taker, and what had happened in the play-off final for Swansea made me even less keen. But Giles was like, 'Well, if you miss, you miss. Life goes on.' As it happened, we had two pens the very next day and I scored them both. For the first one, I was standing there with the ball thinking someone would run up and take it off me. Nobody did, so then I was obliged to take the shot. We ended up beating Cheltenham 4-2. After that, I was the designated penalty taker.

Personally, I had a good season. Especially considering how much the team was struggling. I made 36 appearances in all competitions and scored 15 goals. Not a bad return. Unfortunately, we were relegated. Stockport, Hartlepool and Carlisle all finished on 50 points, and we had 49. It was a real sickener. The last game of the season was away at Leeds in front of 34,000. It was so loud, we couldn't hear each other on the pitch, and ended up losing 3-0. I think it was partly revenge for us beating them earlier in the season at our place.

Boredom can be a big problem for footballers. After training finishes at, say, 1 p.m., we're done. That means we have a lot of free time on our hands. Some guys have crazy hobbies, many are heavily into gaming or gambling. There's plenty of opportunity for mischief. You also have to take into account the pressure we're under. We have to perform every game, knowing that if we don't there's a whole bunch of other players all vying to take our place in the team. Most of the week is spent preparing, mentally and physically, for the game on the Saturday. So as I say, players have various ways to relax and de-stress, or just take their mind off the game for a few minutes. My release was always music.

Because I worked in Northampton but lived in Bristol, I would quite often stay at a hotel; other times I'd stay with Giles Coke. He and I got very close when I was at Northampton, and we still are. I was so grateful to Giles for opening up his home to me. It brought some stability to my life. On the other hand, staying there, and seeing how happy he was with his family, was difficult for me sometimes. I couldn't help but miss my own family, and what I was leaving back home every time I travelled to Northampton. But football was my job, and there are certain things that come with that which you just have to accept. Every job has its pros and cons, and football is no different. I missed Mich and the kids a lot when I was away. But back then I had no idea what it would all lead to, or how close I would come to losing everything.

I was utilising some of the skills I'd learned at St Mary's in my free time and doing a bit of choreography for my younger brother's gigs, just because I loved music so much. It passed the time and took my mind away from football. He used to sing a bit as well. So we would spend a lot of time travelling around the country doing gigs at night clubs and the like. For some reason, one night the champagne came out. I never drink, so I politely declined. But then one of the guys started ripping the piss out of me, asking whether I was a man or a mouse, and then the rest joined in, and soon I was taking stick from all directions. I remember those words coming at me over and over again: 'Are you a man or a mouse?' I should've stuck to my guns, but partly because of the testosterone-driven environment I found myself in most of the time, I just couldn't bring myself to do it. Stupidly, I felt like my masculinity was being questioned.

I thought one glass wouldn't hurt. How wrong I was.

At some point in the evening – I'm not sure of the details – I met a woman in the club. One thing led to another, and we slept together. To me, it was just a bit of fun. Nothing serious. I didn't lie or deceive her. She knew all along I already had a long-term partner in Mich so nothing more was ever going to happen between us. But I couldn't help but feel that she thought there was more to our fling than there actually was.

A couple of weeks later, I was sitting with Giles and his missus in their house when my phone rang. It was this woman from the club. She said she was pregnant. I couldn't believe it. I said there was no way it could be mine. She told me it must be. I was in turmoil. I'm not proud of the lying and cheating. What we did was wrong. No doubt about it. But what came out of it, my son Ajani, is right. He's my second child, born in-between Kamira and Jai. He's seven now.

Me and his mum don't talk. Despite that, I've tried to be a presence in his life. I don't do things half-heartedly. In my opinion you're either all-out or all-in, and when it comes to Ajani I'm all-in. Me and Ajani's mother just don't see eye to eye, and we probably never will.

Do I put some of the blame on the boys I was with? Yes. If they hadn't made me drink that champagne, I never would have done such a despicable thing. But we all have excuses in life. They are easy. What's hard is to man up, accept you made a mistake, and endeavour to put it right. That's why I knew I had to tell Mich. I couldn't have her not knowing, and somebody else having that over her. I wanted us to have a fresh start. But how do you begin a conversation like that? I decided to just come clean, so one day I blurted out everything. I told her I'd met another woman when I was drunk in a club, who was now claiming she was having my baby. Call it woman's intuition or whatever, but Mich said she'd had an inkling that something was up, anyway. Intentionally or unintentionally, I'd been dropping hints which she'd picked up on.

All this came out one Monday. On the following Friday, we were leaving with another couple for New York on holiday. I offered to go by myself, but Mich said, 'We've booked it now, so we'll go together.' It turned out to be the best holiday we've ever been on as a couple. Obviously, our relationship was in serious trouble. But on the holiday we had a lot of time alone to talk things through, with nobody else getting involved. It wouldn't be too much of a stretch to say that New York saved us. Although it was still pretty testing, understandably.

The dynamics of our relationship definitely changed. I'm the first to admit I'm not perfect. Nobody is. But the only way we could both move past what had happened was to accept and learn to live with it. If we'd broken up, it wouldn't be just us we'd hurt, we had kids to think about now too. I had to work hard to rebuild the trust again, and it would be no good Mich throwing it in my face all the time. It was a testing time for all of us. But thankfully we came out the other side of the tunnel even stronger than we were before. True love means you accept each other for what you are, and stand by each other through thick and thin. I'm a very lucky man to have such an understanding partner, and I honestly don't know where I would be without her.

I hadn't told my parents about Ajani at first because I hadn't accepted that Ajani was mine to begin with. When my mum found out, I remember her asking how I could do that to Mich. I love my mum. But like all mummy's boys I fear her, too. I live in south-east London, but, if she calls me from Walthamstow in east London at one in the morning to tell me to go back and put my tea cup away, I'll get in the car and go. That's the power she has over me. My dad is quieter, he's more reasonable. But when it all came out I remember him looking at me and telling me that for the first time in his life he was ashamed of me. He didn't just say it once in the heat of the moment. He said it repeatedly, and each time he said it was like a knife through the heart.

While I tried not to let the off-field stuff affect my game, it weighs on you. But I couldn't let myself just drown in self-pity. I wasn't the first person that had happened to, and I won't be the last. I just had to take it on the chin, admit my mistake, and try to move on. I'm only human, and everyone makes mistakes. That's a given. It's how you come back from them that makes the difference.

• • •

At the beginning of the next season, Northampton struggled again and Stuart Gray was sacked. His assistant, Ian Sampson, was given the job. At a training session, I thought I'd show some support and said to him, 'Don't worry, gaffer. I'm going to go hard for you.' He turned around and said, 'If you're playing.'

That took me by surprise. By then I was the main man, there's no two ways about it. I was twenty-seven, which most people consider the peak years for a striker, I was banging goals in for fun and the fans at Northampton loved me. The first thing Sampson did was sign a new striker, a guy called Courtney Herbert from non-league. He was the quickest kid I'd ever seen. Not the best footballer by a long way, but the quickest. As soon as the kid signed, Sampson relegated me to the bench. I assumed he must have been aiming for a change of tactics or direction in a bid to make his mark as manager. No matter how well I thought I was doing, or how many goals I scored, the fact remained that we'd been relegated with me leading the line. I couldn't argue with that. So young Courtney Herbert came along, took my place in the side, and scored on his debut. That was difficult for me to come to terms with, but from Sampson's perspective it was the best thing that could've happened because it justified his decision-making.

I was stuck on the bench for a couple of games, and then we played Crewe Alex at home. I started the game, and I remember the wind swirling about Sixfields. Somehow we were 0-2 down, but I was winning my headers and having a decent game. As we went into the changing room I remember thinking, the gaffer couldn't possibly justify coming for me, and if he did it would mean it must be some personal issue he had with me. So he started the anticipated rant, and then he stopped, glared at me, and said, 'You, why can't you win your headers? Why aren't you judging the wind?'

That was like a slap in the face, but I'd been half expecting it. I stood up and said, 'What are you talking about? I am winning my headers!'

Suddenly, he puffed out his chest and came walking towards me. I instantly shifted to a self-defence mentality. He poked me in the chest, hard, and I told him, 'Oi, gaffer, stop that.' But he did it again. Then I ripped off my top, marched into the toilet, and punched the door. Not very smart, I know. But it was either punch the door or punch him. So then I'm sitting there with my top off, and the gaffer was like, 'Leave him, if he doesn't want to play we'll get by without him.' But one of the other players said, 'Come on, B, we need you out there.' So I put my top back on, went out for the second half, and within a few minutes I'd scored twice to make it 2-2. I could hear Sampson shouting from the sideline, 'Come on, B! I need one more from you!' I'm thinking '. . . whatever!' After the game, he actually tried to claim credit for the comeback by saying, 'Yeah, sometimes that's what I have to do to get the best out of you.'

Looking back at it now, it seems to be a theme among managers who inherit me. They think '. . . nah.' And I have to prove myself all over again. Sometimes it works, sometimes it doesn't. I ended up playing a lot of games that season, and finished top scorer for the second season in a row with sixteen goals and was voted Northampton's Player of the Year. It got to the point where Sampson had no choice but to play me. His own assistant was telling him that, despite Sampson's personal feelings, they had to keep me because I was so important to the way the team played. The season wasn't a total wash-out. We finished in eleventh place. But it was a bit disappointing because a lot of people expected more from us as we were considered one of the stronger sides in the league and one of the favourites to go up.

It was my decision to leave. I wanted to play at a higher level, it was as simple as that. I was hitting my peak then, and could more than hold my own in League One. I wanted to see how far I could push myself. So towards the end of the season I asked Dean to put some feelers out. He came straight back and said Aberdeen in the Scottish Premier League were interested. They were offering good money too. It was Dean who put the block on that one. A lot of things go through Dean that he knows I won't be into, so he just dismisses them and doesn't even tell me about them. He mentioned the Aberdeen option then told me he couldn't let me commit to them because he knew that if I did, I'd be on the phone to him straightaway asking him why he let me do it. He was like, 'B . . . it's fucking cold up there. You'd hate it!'

BIGGER THAN THE GAME 7

Gillingham (2010–11)
Northampton Town (2011–12)

There have only been a couple of times in my life when, as a man, I've completely lost my shit and broken down. I'm not going to say one of those times was when I just learned how cold it was in Scotland. I kind of suspected that to be the case before Dean even told me. This wasn't even football-related. Some things are more important than football. Any dad will tell you that nothing tugs on your heartstrings like something terrible happening to one of your kids. That summer, while I was on holiday in Atlanta, I had a call from Mich. She explained our daughter Kamira had an abscess around her belly button, and she was taking her to the doctor's. It seemed routine enough. The trip to the doctor was more for peace of mind than any genuine concern. But they took one look at Kamira and said she needed an operation immediately. It was serious. So Mich called me again from the hospital and let me talk to Kamira. I asked her how she was feeling, and she said, 'I'm fine, Daddy. I have to have an operation. I can't eat anything, so I'm very hungry. But I'm being tough, and I haven't cried.'

And that was the part where I lost my shit and broke down in the hotel lobby. I just felt so helpless. I was abroad. I couldn't hold her or do anything to make what she was going through any better. The only thing that pulled me together was my brother Yemi telling me it would be bad for her if Kamira heard me crying. I was supposed to be the provider, the strong one. I should be setting an example for her to follow.

Thankfully, they didn't even have to operate in the end, but the experience lit a fire in me. Before I had kids, I wasn't a very emotional guy. I know it's something everybody says, but having kids changes you. Your priorities swing on a dime. Suddenly, it's not all about you, and it affects you in the most bizarre ways. Some days I'll be watching TV with them, some kid's story about a homeless orphaned unicorn or some shit, and I'll find myself welling up. I have to shake it off and ask myself what the fuck I'm doing. I can't go crying at cartoons . . .

I eventually signed for Gillingham under Andy Hessenthaler, who'd made his name as a powerhouse midfielder for the Gills and Watford. They were also in League Two, having just been relegated, but our squad that season should really have dominated. We were far too good for League Two with the likes of Barry Fuller (Stevenage, Barnet), Kevin Maher (Oldham Athletic, Southend United), Matt Lawrence (Fulham, Millwall, Crystal Palace) and Jack Payne (Peterborough United, Blackpool) in the side. I scored on my debut at home against Cheltenham, but other than that the first couple of months there were quite hard for me. I was doing all the right things, but it just wasn't the same. I hadn't really achieved anything at Priestfield Stadium, so I wasn't getting the same kind of love from the fans as I was used to getting at Northampton, and I wasn't getting the same kind of service from the lads on the pitch, either. I'm not saying it was anything less. It was just different. The team had a different way of playing, so it was a period of adjustment. I was still bedding in. I was playing a lot of matches, but not getting on the score sheet nearly often enough. That bothered me because I usually grab at least a goal every two or three games. As a striker, if you go six, seven, eight games without a goal you know you're on borrowed time and it starts to eat away at you and erode your confidence.

Not scoring many goals was countered by the fact that we usually managed to keep it tight at the back. But there was the odd game where we'd just go to pieces and ship goals like nobody's business, which was frustrating. We lost 5-4 at Bury and 7-4 at Accrington Stanley. I scored a penalty there, but it was one of those games where everyone seemed to score. Embarrassingly, we went out of the Football League Trophy early, and were dumped out of the FA Cup in the first round by non-league Dover Athletic who beat us 2-0 on our own patch.

I'd had enough, and asked Dean to try to sort a loan move out back to Northampton for me. I was generally bitching a lot. Rather than focusing on the club, my mind was elsewhere. I just didn't feel comfortable, and actually went to the gaffer and apologised to him. But then Cody McDonald (Norwich City, AFC Wimbledon), who we had on loan from Norwich, got fit and we just started tearing things up. We became a formidable partnership. I scored eleven that season, he banged in about twenty-five and I assisted half of them. From the end of January to the middle of April we went sixteen games unbeaten.

As I said, I've never been a drinker. I'm usually just high on life. But after we got knocked out of the League Cup at Norwich in the first round, the gaffer gave us four or five days off so I flew out to Atlanta with my two brothers and my best mate, Regal. Whenever my brothers and I go abroad and people ask us if we play American football, we always say, 'Yeah, we play for a team called London Dungeon. You should come and check us out!' It was Thanksgiving, so we went to a club. I'd just walked in through the door when some guy barged me in the back. Unlike me and my brothers, my friend Regal isn't a big guy, but he switches on a sixpence. He saw me and this dude go face to face so he grabbed the guy's hands. Seconds later, about eighteen bouncers were on us. Little did I know but the guy who had barged me was one of them. The next thing I knew, one of the bouncers literally picked Regal up and carried him out. All you could see were his little legs pumping. We took the piss out of him for years for that.

Meanwhile, I was telling myself to stay calm and not to switch, otherwise they'd kick me out too after I'd just paid $60 to get in the VIP area. By now the whole club was watching, and I was trying to talk everyone down while I was being held by a bouncer who was trying to march me out of the place but he had to give up. I didn't even have to throw a single punch, he knew what was up. I always try to be diplomatic in those situations. Getting violent rarely solves anything. Especially when you're a visitor on someone else's patch. Then the police came, and we all found ourselves outside thinking, 'What happened?' We were in the place for fifteen minutes tops, and ten minutes of that was us getting thrown out.

The following year, we went back to the same club, only this time there were nine of us. We had the same drama, but it ended very differently. We all got separated in the club, and we heard this bird call, which is something we used to do on the estate. It was like, 'Avengers assemble!' We all raced over from different parts of the club to where it was kicking off with the bouncers, and the one who had marched me out on our first visit saw me, and ran to the back of the group. He didn't want to know. In the end, the bouncers threw out this other guy who'd started everything and let me and my boys stay there so finally justice was done.

Despite our run of good form in the second half of the season, we lost our last two games and eventually finished eighth in the league. My old employers Torquay took the last play-off place on goal difference, only to lose the final against Stevenage. With promotion going begging, the Gills had to make cut-backs. They didn't renew a lot of players' contracts, and the ones they did offer terms, the money was so bad it was an insult. In an attempt to avoid any confrontation, they were sent out by post. I got my contract, and I thought to myself, 'There's no way I can sign this.' Not when I knew I could get more money at another club. Who in their right mind would?

We played my previous employers Northampton Town twice that season, losing away and beating them at home. Ian Sampson had been sacked by then, and I remember his old assistant, who was still there, telling me how hard he tried to persuade the club to keep me. Gary Johnson got the manager's job. I've not been re-signed by another manager other than Kenny Jackett, but whatever happens with them, I always seem to have a good relationship with chairmen. I got on really well with Huw Jenkins at Swansea and Paul Scally at Gillingham, while David Cardoza at Northampton Town liked me so much he ended up signing me twice.

I sat down to have a talk with Gary Johnson about going back to Northampton, a club I still had a lot of affection for, and initially found him very sharp and abrupt. It was a young team – I think the average age was about twenty-two – and they responded well to Gary's manner. I'd been around a long time by then, so I didn't appreciate it too much. Another factor that may have played a part in Johnson's attitude with me that day was the fact that, on Dean's advice, I was deliberately acting as if I wasn't interested. He thought that if the club was under the impression that I wasn't keen on going back, they might make me a better offer in order to tempt me.

What I did appreciate were the lengths the club went to in order to re-sign me. It made me feel valued. They offered me a very good contract, especially for League Two, and I was determined to earn it. People say 'never go back' but I had good times at Northampton. In both my full seasons I had been top goalscorer, and the fans were always amazing. So why not? My mentality is that if I enjoyed doing something, I'm probably going to enjoy doing it again. The manager had changed. But most of the players were the same, the fans were the same, and the stadium was the same. So for me, it was a no-brainer.

One of the most surreal episodes I've ever experienced in football was my first game of the season when I saw a WELCOME BACK, BAYO! banner in the crowd. Every time I touched the ball, a huge roar went up around Sixfields. It reminded me of the kind of cult hero status Lee Trundle had at Swansea, where he would get cheered just for flicking the ball out of play and reiterated the fact that I saw that club as an extended family. They took me in when I was desperate, and I always wanted to show my gratitude for that. Of course, the best way for me to do that was on the pitch. At most clubs I would go though cycles, where I played well for ten games, was average for ten, and bad for ten. I can't remember having a terrible game for Northampton but I'm sure there were a few bad ones. Of course, there were games where I didn't get on the score sheet, and games where the team collectively didn't perform, but even then I was always happy with my contribution.

I soon found out that one of the root problems at the club was that there was a divide in the dressing room. Things were very cliquey, and literally black and white. The black players all flocked together, and the white players did the same, with very little interaction between the two groups. That kind of situation is never good. I believe that team spirit surpasses ability, but you have to work hard to nurture it.

I have tried to use my stature as a positive, especially in recent years. These days I walk into a changing room and let everyone know, especially the younger players, that I'm there for them. In my mind we are all soldiers together, fighting on the same side. And every time we step onto the pitch, we're going to war together. Managers often look at me as someone who can galvanise a changing room and lead the troops, and I'm more than happy to do my bit, especially in the lower leagues where experience is absolutely vital. I try to promote solidarity and togetherness at every opportunity, because it makes a much stronger team. I am very aware of the influence I have in the changing room. People listen when I speak.

One thing I've always hated are players who talk for the manager. You don't hear a peep out of them, and suddenly they go, 'Yeah boys, let's go in for the kill! Come on!' You ask yourself what suddenly brought that outburst on. Then all becomes clear when the manager walks in just as they are saying it. You instantly know what kind of person they are. They are putting on a front, in the hope it will win them favour. What they often fail to realise is that everyone sees them for what they really are: showboaters. When shit gets real, they're probably nowhere to be found. Me, because I'm so conscious of my influence and don't want to be seen as one of those guys, I do my talking when the manager isn't there. I will often have a one-on-one with the younger players. I let them know if I'm angry about something, but I won't make a big deal of it. I don't do anything just for plaudits.

In my opinion, the game has become far too safe. Modern footballers are too spoiled and molly-coddled. Everyone walks on eggshells around them, afraid of the consequences if they get upset. We need to get some of the grit back, and accept that it's okay to be angry sometimes. Especially if it helps win games, which is why we're all there. I felt that, because of his abrupt demeanour, Gary Johnson could intimidate some of the youngsters. I was about thirty-one by then, so especially with such a young squad, I was automatically considered a senior player and I took that responsibility on board. We would have weekly team meetings after training without him being there, just so the players could get things off their chests. A few of them were afraid to speak out when he was around. It did cross my mind that the gaffer may have thought I was undermining him at times. But that really wasn't the case. I was doing everything I could to help him and the club.

On the pitch, we struggled badly that season. From October through to February, we played eighteen league games and lost thirteen of them. During one game, I looked across at Gary Johnson and he was just sitting in the dugout with his head in his hands. He wasn't ranting or raving, or giving instructions like he would normally be doing. I'm not sure if his health problems that have been recently documented were there at the time, but it just looked like he'd run out of ideas and given up. It seemed as though all his drive and enthusiasm was gone.

We slipped to rock bottom of the league, and that led to him leaving by mutual consent. It was probably the best solution for all parties. His assistant, David Lee, took over for one game, and he made Michael Jacobs (Derby County, Wolverhampton Wanderers, Wigan Athletic) captain. He turned out to be a great player, but was barely twenty at the time and I remember thinking that was a bit strange. Lee's reasoning was that it would give the fans a boost, but I can't help thinking that surely I would have been a better choice for the armband. I was far more experienced, and had a presence around the club. As it was, that game turned out to be a 7-2 home defeat by Shrewsbury, so in the aftermath I was glad he hadn't made me captain!

Not long after that game, the club brought in Aidy Boothroyd. My first impression of him was that he was a great talker. He could inspire a team, there was no doubt about that. He'd accomplished things, the pinnacle being winning promotion to the Premier League and claiming a place in the FA Cup semi-final with Watford, so was a big name. He arrived just before Christmas. With my family being religious, we get together every Christmas Day and pray. But because we had a game on Boxing Day, Boothroyd told all the players he wanted us in for training at 5.30 on Christmas Day. I explained the situation to him and he told me that even though everyone else would be going in, he would give me the day off. He said that there are certain players you have to treat differently to get the best out of them and I was one of those players. I thought okay, great. But then he said he wouldn't be starting me in the Boxing Day game. I wasn't going to argue with him, so I just agreed and thanked him for giving me the day off.

I didn't start another game for over six weeks. Boothroyd told me he wanted me to get fitter, and asked me to come in on Thursdays for double training sessions. That suited me, because Thursday and Friday I would stay in Northampton, but on Monday and Tuesday I would drive back to London because if we didn't have a midweek game, we had Wednesday off. This went on for six or seven weeks, and I started to worry that he just didn't fancy me. A reporter asked him why I wasn't playing, and Boothroyd said something like, 'Well, when B's in the team we talk about him, and when he's not in the team we still talk about him.' That made me think he might have issues with me that went above and beyond football.

• • •

Most football fans will be familiar with my name because of what I've achieved on the pitch. But something that raised my profile outside the game, especially among those who play video games, is my association with the *FIFA* franchise. The first I ever heard about it was when my best friend, Regal, gave me a call and told me I was in a KSI video which blew up on the Internet. At the time, I had absolutely no social media presence whatsoever. I had no Twitter, no Instagram, no Facebook page, nothing. I had no desire to even get involved. It wasn't something I wanted to think about. I knew the *FIFA* games, but I hadn't even seen this video Regal was talking about. This is where I should give a big shout out to YouTube sensation KSI, who started the ball rolling, and opened my eyes to the power of social media. He posted this video about 'beast players' in the *FIFA* game, and did a segment about me. I didn't even play *FIFA*. I was in the *Pro Evo* camp for a while, but had stopped playing that, too. I was never really much into gaming, especially after the kids came along. This KSI video was saying things like, 'Akinfenwa can lift whole planets!' and made a big deal of me being the strongest footballer in the world. By the time I saw it, KSI's video had had over two million views, but even then I didn't think too much of it. It was just a funny video.

A while later, one of my brothers went on Twitter and saw that someone had made an account in my name, and they had over 2,000 followers. So I went and had a look, and saw that whoever had made this fake account was having conversations with people as if he or she were me. That's taking liberties. I saw one convo where they were chatting with Danny Spiller, my old Gillingham teammate, about training. My brother started saying that this person had all these followers, who all thought he or she was me, and were obviously interested in my life and what I had to say, so why didn't I make my own Twitter account and try to capitalise on it a little?

I thought it wouldn't hurt, so that day I made an account

and within an hour I had as many followers as the fake me. I saw KSI was up to something, so I commented that I'd seen the video he did, and he was like, 'Oh my days, it's The Beast!' He was awestruck because he was talking to a footballer, and I was awestruck because I'd discovered this whole world full of massive potential in which he was already a main player. He was only seventeen or eighteen at the time, but was very tech-savvy and already a huge YouTube celebrity. Those people are like the new rock stars, and him just talking about me certified me and gave me some kudos with the younger generation. When he suggested us making a video together I jumped at the opportunity, just because it sounded like something new and exciting, not even knowing that he had over seven million subscribers to his YouTube channel.

From that point on, I took an active interest in social media. The next step was making an Instagram account. For a long time, I wanted to make a distinction between my footballing life and my personal life. So I had two accounts on both Twitter and Instagram, one for my private life, and one for football-related stuff. Dele warned me I would never be able to maintain that attitude, and the four accounts. He was right. In the end I deleted my 'private' accounts and merged the two into one. Or the four into two. At some point it dawned on me what an amazing title 'Strongest Player in *FIFA*' is to have. By the way, if you search my name and 'FIFA' in YouTube today, you'll get over 88,000 hits. That's not how many views they've had, that's how many videos have been posted.

When things started to take off for me on social media, my brother Dele really came to the forefront and it was at this time of our lives I saw his amazing business brain. I always knew it of course, but here he was able to put it into practice. He is my right-hand man. I chat to him every day. We've always had that mad bond, always able to motivate one another from the gym to business. I have watched him evolve from the start of Beast Mode and managing me to now where he runs the operation and knows the business better than anyone. I wouldn't be able to do half the things I do without him. I'm very lucky. And it all got started really after we had a sit-down chat in Wood Green and discussed how we could maximise it. That's how the whole Beast Mode thing came around. My nickname on the pitch was The Beast, and we started to think how we could marry that with the 'FIFA's strongest man' stuff, and my growing social media presence. Pretty soon, it developed beyond a few catchy sayings and slogans like 'Beast Mode On' and 'BMO' into an entire ethos. In a nutshell, the whole idea behind it is to never let anyone tell you that you can or can't do something for whatever reason. The people who do that and try to keep you down are, more often than not, projecting their own shortcomings and insecurities onto you. Don't let them. Something people have always said about me is I that I'm too big to play football. Fuck them. If I'd listened to the haters I never would have achieved anything, and I wouldn't have the life I have now. The only thing Dele and I wanted to achieve with it all back then was to have it mean something. We didn't even know what at the time. We just wanted to create something with a positive message and have people buy into it.

My first ever Beast Mode-related tweet was when I was stuck in traffic and I said, 'This guy's trying to give me road rage. He must be in beast mode #BMO.' After that, I used the same hashtag on every tweet, and soon it became synonymous with my name. I have a lot to thank KSI for. Until he started making videos about me, I had no idea about the social media world. I didn't even know I was the strongest player in *FIFA*. It was only after all that came to light that I was able to manoeuvre certain things around and take advantage.

I was never into designer clothes. In truth, in the beginning I never envisioned BMO as a brand. It was more a case of, 'Let's put the BMO slogan out there and see what happens.' It was my brother who first suggested using it on a T-shirt, that being the most tangible and easily accessible thing. Who doesn't wear T-shirts? They cover the whole spectrum: young, old, male, female, big, small. He had a hook-up with someone who had done

T-shirts for his shows before, so we got a design printed up in two colours, black and white, set up a website to sell them through, and I started promoting them on social media. I remember saying, 'It won't hurt to try it. If it doesn't work out, it doesn't work out. Nothing ventured, nothing gained.' But deep down I was thinking, 'Who's going to pay money just to have the BMO logo on one of their T-shirts? Surely it can't be that simple.'

The very first design we put out was a little dig at the people who doubted me. It said, 'Too Big to Play Football, Ha Ha.' They started selling immediately. I remember telling my mum that there was nothing better than making money while you're sleeping. We had a PayPal account connected to my brother's phone, and we were walking down the street listening to the notifications of payment coming through. Ding! £25. Ding! £25. Ding! £25.

After a while, I thought perhaps the 'Too Big to Play Football, Ha Ha' design was a bit too specific and oriented towards me personally, so we started to think of designs that were more generic and applicable to a wider market. That's when we started doing 'Beast Mode On' and the rest. After the T-shirts came the hoodies and baseball caps, and then we started doing ladies' and kids' wear. Everything just sort of spiralled. Now, we even do branded cushions.

The Northampton fans really got behind the Beast Mode thing. They were a huge part of why it took off. But I don't think any of it sat well with Boothroyd, and the bigger it got the more it unsettled him. One of the first things he did in the January transfer window was bring in Saido Berahino on loan from West Brom. He was only about eighteen then, but the kid could play. He scored a few goals in his time at Northampton. If he had re-signed I might never have got back in the team, but he moved to Brentford and the gaffer was virtually forced to put me back in. I went on a good goalscoring run, and Boothroyd was always trying to take the credit for it. He was telling reporters that when he went there I wasn't in shape, and he was the one who got me match-fit. If he wants to take plaudits for it, fine. He was the one who got me in for double sessions, that much is true. But he never once said anything like that to my face because he knew I'd argue it. The first I heard about it was in the press. It's funny how when you're on a good run there's always someone trying to take credit for it, but when you're on a bad run, you're on your own.

People started calling him Hoofroyd, because of the route-one football he was playing. That was ironic because he was the first one to tell me about horseshoes. Between the corner flags and the edge of the box there are squares, and he would tell players to play balls into that area to turn defenders and make them play the game in their own half. In all my years in football, that was the first time I heard the term 'horseshoes'. Boothroyd was a huge advocate. He didn't like the Hoofroyd label, and tried his best to get away from it. I've always believed you should be who you are. If you like playing direct football, fine, just be good at it, and don't try to dress it up or change your style to please others. Boothroyd liked runners, but he also liked direct football, and that's what I'm best at. By hook or by crook, Boothroyd stabilised the club and after a shaky start results improved and we finished the season in twentieth position, well clear of the relegation zone. I was playing regularly and scoring goals, and I still had another year to run on my contract. There was a genuine feeling around the club that with Hoofroyd, sorry, Boothroyd, at the helm, the club could go places.

• • •

Mich always said she wanted four kids. By this time we already had Kamira and Jai, so then we had Kaliyah. Thank God, I was around for the birth this time so there were no dramas. I was now in my thirties, so I knew how to handle the whole thing better. I always go out of my way to make sure my kids aren't spoiled. They never go without, but they aren't spoiled, either. My own upbringing is the model for that. By the time Kaliyah arrived, as a family we'd gone through the bad times, and were then on a sound financial footing. It was still a bit precarious. Being a footballer always is. But we were in a much better situation than after I'd broken my leg and we had Kamira.

Kaliyah is the diva of the family. She's very sassy, and loves wearing princess dresses to school. She's always had me wrapped around her little finger. I actually fear for the guys she's going to meet later in life. She's going to rip out their hearts and wear them on a chain around her neck. It's probably my fault. Because Kamira was the first, we did a lot of things like boxing and sit-ups. She loves it. But with Kaliyah, I never did any of that so she's such a girly girl.

8 OFF AND ON THE PITCH

Northampton Town (2012–13)
Gillingham (2013–14)

During the close season, the gaffer sat me down and told me he was bringing in Clive Platt (Rochdale, MK Dons, Colchester United) who'd just been released from Boothroyd's old club Coventry, and he wasn't being brought in to sit on the bench. A lot of people might have thought Platty and I were rivals because we played in the same position. But nothing could be further from the truth. We were, and are, good friends, and want each other to succeed both on the pitch and off it. He's a couple of years older than me, and I always look up to my elders. I've never really had a problem with another player simply because they play in my position because ultimately, the players don't pick the team. It's not our decision. I learned a lot from Platty. He was one of the people telling me to go out there on match day, express myself, and never be afraid to be me.

We also signed Louis Moult (Motherwell) and Alex Nicholls (Walsall, Exeter City, Barnet), both strikers. Despite this, I was still getting games and scoring well when I had the chance. If I was on the bench, more often than not the fans would call me on. In November we played Accrington Stanley away and I scored my first ever hat-trick in a 4-2 win. That January, Gillingham came in for me. I knew Boothroyd wasn't going to offer me a new contract so I asked him to let me leave, as it would be easier and more beneficial to me if I negotiated a deal while I was still under contract at another club. At first, he asked me to wait until he found a replacement, then he changed his mind and said, 'If I let you go and we fall away, I'm going to get it in the neck from the fans.' So I was stuck there.

When Aidy Boothroyd brought Clarke Carlisle (Blackpool, QPR, Leeds United) to Northampton initially on loan from Burnley, it sparked one of the weirdest bromances ever. The first thing Boothroyd did was make him captain. It was a masterstroke, because Carlisle is probably the best skipper I've ever played under. What made him so good? He never stopped talking. He was always organising and encouraging people. It didn't matter what was happening on the pitch, whether either of us was having a good game or a bad game, you always felt like he was beside you. You never felt alone, and you can't underestimate how important that is as a player. His diet was coffee and chocolate, but he was as ripped as hell, and was the most intelligent person I'd ever met. He's also very humble, has impeccable manners, and even calls everyone he meets 'sir'. He's the person who taught me that when you meet someone you should shake their hand, look them in the eye, and tell them your full name because then they never forget who you are. It's a small thing, but something I've always remembered. Life is a lesson, and I always try to learn from the people I meet.

We clicked on just about every level. We got each other. I think one of the key aspects was the contrast between us. I had a decent enough education at my comprehensive school, and consider myself pretty articulate, but he's on another level, using words with about twenty syllables in them. The rest of us would be looking at him as if he was from a different planet. I've never really hung out much with other footballers in my social time. I've always been with my brothers, and when the season finishes, football is over for me until the next season starts. Mich is also good friends with Clarke's wife. They always say that we care more about each other than we do about them. I'd argue against that. But I'd have to, wouldn't I?

Northampton had one of the best home records in the division, until April rolled around and we played York City. They beat us 0-2, which ended our hopes of automatic promotion. The last game of the season was Barnet at home. We were already in the play-offs but they needed a win to stay up. We were drawing 0-0, and I went on as sub. Edgar Davids (Ajax, Juventus, Tottenham Hotspur and Holland) came running up and, given the situation, asked me not to do anything. I thought he was having a joke and said, 'Okay, cool.'

Later in the match, I was part of the move that led to our first goal, and Davids came up again. 'I thought I told you not to do anything!' he said. He was getting very intense. I was thinking, 'What do you want me to do?' They'd beaten us 4-0 earlier in the season, and hadn't shown us any mercy then. We scored again not long after, and it turned out to be one of the best thirty-minute cameos of my entire career. I won Player of the Month, and because we were sponsored by Audi, they would give you the use of one of their cars for the weekend. I had an A7, which was about £65,000 worth of car. We decided to drive it up to Sheffield to watch the boxing. We were ringside for a great fight night. Amir Khan beat Julio Diaz, Deontay Wilder knocked out Audley Harrison in the first round, and it was Anthony Ogogo's pro debut. We all wore Beast Mode tops to the fight, then changed to BMO tops (more classy!) to go out after the show. I was in a club, and some dude by himself just started giving my younger brother lip. I went over to see what was what, and tripped over right in the middle of the dance floor. Smooth. I got up just in time to see my older brother stick one on this guy, and then the bouncers came over and ushered us out. I remember someone telling me to turn my top inside out, in case the bouncers made the connection and recognised me. I didn't want the bad press to come back on the BMO brand. Generally, we don't get into too much trouble when we go out. Our size alone is a big deterrent!

We finished in sixth place, and to make it even worse, Gillingham did the double over us and won the league. We drew Cheltenham Town in the play-offs, and beat them home and away to set up a final against Bradford City, who were our bogey team that season. Up until then we'd played them four times in all competitions and not beaten them once. A day or two before the game, the gaffer rented out a cinema and we had a team outing to go and watch *Fast & Furious 6*. As we were walking toward the cinema, he pulled me to one side and said he'd be playing Platty in the final. Now I love Platty. He's my boy. But he'd been out injured for six weeks or so and hadn't even trained properly. I'd banged in seventeen goals up to that point, and was clear top scorer. I just couldn't see how Boothroyd could justify not playing me. When I questioned his decision, he just said he had 'a feeling'. I always thought it was more of a power play on his part, to show everyone who was boss. Managers always have their favourites, and it just so happened that Platty was one of his and I wasn't. Whatever his thinking was, it didn't work because we were 3-0 down after about twenty minutes. Andy King, his assistant, told me to warm up and I just said, 'What for?'

Andy King and I were at loggerheads all the time. He used to say to me, 'B, you're great at what you do. But for some reason, when you're in the team, it doesn't work.' And he would be very direct and upfront about it, which I can accept. Then we would have a back-and-forth discussion and at the end of it I'd go away asking myself why it wasn't working and what adjustments I could make in my own game to benefit the team. We are men in this football world, and I firmly believe we should be real with each other.

A criticism a lot of managers seem to have is that when I'm on the pitch, my teammates see me and automatically go long. But I always think that's on them, it's their choice, so why am I getting it in the neck? If they don't listen to what the gaffer says, it's them who needs a talking to not me. My managers also notice when other teams double up on me and bring that up a lot, saying I'm being marked out of the game. I'm not going to lie, it's almost impossible to play when you have two markers on you all the time. But if they are doubling up on me, that must surely mean we have an extra man elsewhere on the pitch, so why isn't the manager focusing on that? Instead the manager invariably says that because I can't get the better of two defenders, I should come out of the team. It makes no sense to me.

I ended up going on in about the 68th minute, and by then the game had slipped away. That defeat hurt. I felt like Northampton Town was my club, and at times I carried it on my shoulders. I felt responsible. It's the only club I've ever been at where win or lose the supporters would hold me accountable and be tweeting me afterwards asking me to explain certain things, or just to have a go if we hadn't played well. Most of the time they were civil and respectful, but it's always best to stay off Twitter after a defeat. To go out like that was soul destroying.

• • •

After we lost in the play-off final, Clarke Carlisle announced his retirement. As close as we were, I had no idea what he was going through at the time. Boothroyd must have known more, because he would often cover for Clarke by telling the squad he wasn't going in that day. He had a lot of media stuff going on at the time, so none of us thought anything of it. In retrospect, though, it was obvious something was terribly wrong. Once, he turned up for training and couldn't get out of his car. A couple of years later, when I heard he'd had an 'accident', I sent his wife a message and asked her what had happened. She told me he'd tried to kill himself. They didn't want the public to know at the time, so she made me promise not to tell anybody. I drove up to visit him at the clinic he was staying at in Sheffield. The joke, if you can call it that, was the only reason he survived being hit by a lorry was because he was as big as a lorry. The first thing he did when he saw me was ask if I'd brought him any chicken. I hadn't. But I had taken my mother's bible, which is pretty special because it has soil from Jerusalem in it. We read some psalms together.

When we talked, I asked him to make me understand why he would do such a thing. I just didn't get it. He had retired from the game, but was still relevant. He was building a second career as an ITV and Sky Sports pundit, and to date is the only footballer ever to appear on *Question Time*. Worst of all, he had kids, and he was going to kill himself on Christmas Day. That would tarnish Christmas for them forever. I tried to convince him that the reason he failed in his suicide attempt was because God wasn't ready to take him. He still had work to do in this life. He said, 'Look, depression is a disease. Just because you can't see it, it doesn't mean it's not there.'

Apparently it was all because he'd been caught drink-driving, and it was going to come out in the press. Other things may have contributed, but that was what pushed him over the edge. So he parked up his Mercedes and just stepped out into the road. I stayed with him for about three hours. Then, when I went, I left the bible with him and said he can give it back when he's ready. We still talk now. We have one of those relationships where we might not talk for a few months, then one of us will pick up the phone and we'll sound like we talk every day. He was having problems paying his bills for a time, and I helped him out with that. He paid me back like clockwork, and slowly but surely he got his life back together.

• • •

When I go to away grounds it sometimes takes me twenty minutes to get back to the coach from leaving the changing room after the game because of the fan base I have. I always have to stay behind for a while to take selfies and sign autographs, or just exchange a bit of banter with the fans. I get much more attention than most League Two players. If I send out a tweet or an Instagram message, it gets noticed. At the last count I had 708,000 Instagram followers, and almost 200,000 Twitter followers. That's a combined reach of almost a million, which is a lot more than most lower-division clubs. Managers know that, and they either try to utilise it or just accept it. But the thing was, Boothroyd didn't sign me. He inherited me. And he has an ego, if you know what I mean. There's nothing wrong with that. I have an ego, too. We all have. It's how you manage it that makes all the difference. For example, when he first came in and the club was bottom of League Two I remember him telling me that he had aspirations of managing England. I was like, 'What?' I have nothing against people being ambitious and setting goals for themselves, but you have to be realistic and, at the time, he was the manager of a struggling League Two club. However, a couple of years later he got to be the England Under-21 manager, which is only one step away from the top job.

His ego isn't the reason I don't like him. The reason for that is this: after I left I heard rumours he'd been joking to people that 'Well, B told me he was trying to lose weight. But when I looked in his car, there were McDonald's and KFC wrappers all over the place. Then I tried to get him in for extra training and he refused.' That isn't what happened. Not even close. I thought, 'Look, don't say things about me now. Especially when I'm not there to defend myself.' That's how I knew beyond reasonable doubt that it was personal. He dismissed my capabilities, drummed me out of the club, then slandered me afterwards to try to justify his decision when I wasn't even there. If he'd said he'd found loads of Nando's wrappers, it would be something. But no, he told everyone I'd been eating McDonald's and KFC. I don't even like McDonald's and KFC!

I was advised not to speak out about it publicly, because it wouldn't really have done me any good. I didn't have the platform then that I do now. I was doing a fortnightly column for the *Daily Mail* and I did say some things about it there. But that was more a reaction to these outlandish claims he was making about me. I didn't think it through very well. What I wanted to put across was that you live and die by your decisions. If I met Boothroyd now, I'd be cordial, because that's the kind of man I am. He's not a factor in my life any more, same as I'm not a factor in his. He lasted another half a season at Northampton before getting sacked, leaving them rock bottom of the league. That was when he took the England Under-21 job. In fairness, he's done well for them, but I don't think they'll be offering him the top job any time soon.

When the season finished, I signed with Gillingham, who'd just been promoted to League One. I was still devastated at not getting Northampton promoted, but I'd done my best and it was time to try to let it go and put it behind me. My old strike partner Cody McDonald was still at the Gills, and they were being managed by Martin Allen who, hands down, is by far the craziest manager I have ever played under. He's known in the game as 'Mad Dog', and believe me, he's earned that title. The moment I arrived at training, he looked at me and said, 'I can see you like chicken.'

A bit taken aback, I said, 'Well, yeah. I do. I'm never going to deny that.'

So then he stood there looking around and going, 'All right, all right, all right,' in this funny voice. Later on, he asked me to pick up the bibs after training. I was like, '... what? I'm supposed to be a senior player around here.' But I was prepared for that one because Gills skipper Adam Barrett (Southend United, Bournemouth, Mansfield Town) had told me moments before that he was going to test me, and to just go along with whatever the man said. So Martin Allen asked me to pick up the training bibs and take them to him and I just went, 'Right, let's go!' and clapped my hands to show my enthusiasm. The confused expression on his face was hilarious, because he'd obviously expected me to protest.

He had a habit of calling me into his office to tell me what we'd be doing that day and discuss tactics in the mornings before training. I appreciated the fact that he wanted to share that stuff with me and get me involved, but I wasn't a coach, I was a player. I didn't need to know all that. To make matters even more bizarre, the Martin Allen that used to call me into his office every morning was completely different from the Martin Allen that would then be at training. It was so Jekyll and Hyde. Not long after I arrived, I started hearing rumours that he might be getting sacked. He'd just got the club promoted, so I thought that was a bit odd. But apparently there was certain behind-the-scenes stuff going on that the chairman and various other influential people at the club weren't happy about. I was new, so I was just trying to keep my head down and take all this in.

We clashed almost straight away. One of the main reasons the Gills brought me in was because I'd scored about nine goals from set-pieces in my last season at Northampton and the Gills thought they could benefit from that. So in training, Martin Allen asked me to stand in a certain position so we could do a few drills. I explained that wasn't where I'd been positioned when I got all the goals, I was coming from deeper and arriving late in the box. Then he said something like, 'Oh, everyone stop what you're doing and listen to Bayo. It seems he's the expert!' If we'd carried on working together much longer than we did, I'm pretty sure 'Adebayo Akinfenwa just punched Martin Allen in the face' would've come up on the Sky Sports ticker line.

He was another manager who liked high-energy runners. But he signed me, knowing that wasn't what I brought to the team. I was thirty-two years-old and I weighed over sixteen stone. I couldn't run channels and turn defenders if my life depended on it. In fact, I've probably never run a channel in my life. That's just not my game. We did a training session which was purposely based around kicking the ball into channels and he would be saying, 'Don't worry, boys, the big man will go after it!'

Another weird thing about Martin Allen is that when he talks, he takes off his clothes. I'm serious. He'll start with a suit and tie, and by the end of it he'll be sitting there with his belly hanging out. There were times I felt more like a coach than a player under him. During one game, we were winning and he asks me what I thought we needed to do. I told him I thought we didn't need to do anything. We were doing everything right. Then the other team equalised, so I said I thought we were dropping too deep, and then Allen got riled. He was shouting, 'Arsène Wenger now, are you? Hmm? Arsène bloody Wenger?' I was like, 'But you asked me, and then you mug me off!' That was one of the times I came close to hitting him. I had to leave the bench and do a warm-up to clear my head.

We didn't win any of the first eight matches. I remember being on the pitch, looking over at this guy everyone said I was going to like, and he'd just be going mental. Off the field, you could have a decent conversation with him. But otherwise, he was a complete mentalist. People say because he was under so much pressure, I didn't get the real Martin Allen, which may or may not be true. I got the impression that people above him in the club were telling Martin Allen to play me and Cody together because we were a proven strike partnership and the team were struggling for goals. It was just logical. We played Crawley Town away, and for the first and only time in my career, I got hooked off before half-time. It was something like the 32nd minute. I was so pissed off and embarrassed that I wanted to smash up the changing room, and made my feelings known to the point that the rest of the lads were scared to come in. We still ended up losing the game 3-2 so whatever grand plan Allen had blatantly hadn't worked. Later, he came out in the press and said he should have made the changes after the last game, where we'd also performed badly, and not waited until the Crawley match had started.

I always think football matters should stay in-house. It's a matter of respect. The world doesn't need to know our business. Furthermore, as players, you have to accept the manager's decisions and just get on with it, whether you agree with them or not. That's why they are managing and you are playing. But looking back, I really should have taken issue with him about some of his dealings with the press. There was a team meeting not long afterwards and Myles Weston (Notts County, Brentford, Southend United), who is now at Wycombe Wanderers with me, had a go at him for throwing people under the bus. He said, 'When we win, it's "us". But when we lose, it's always "you", and you single someone out for criticism.' It wasn't doing anyone any favours.

A couple of weeks later, we played Crewe Alex. Before the match, the gaffer had asked me to sit on the bench with him and keep him calm. So we go 2-0 up in this game, and one of our players played a dodgy back pass. Martin Allen jumped up in his seat and started waving his arms about like a madman. He was going absolutely mental. So I grabbed him, and sat him back down. I'm saying, 'We're 2-0 up. There's no need to lose it. We can afford one mistake. Even if Crewe score, we'll still be winning.' He calmed down a bit, but then asked me to go down and encourage the boys. I was like, 'What? We're 2-0 up. We're doing fine. Trying to encourage them now might cause more harm than good.' To keep the peace, I did as he asked, went down to the touchline, and started clapping and shouting at the boys. The Crewe players started looking at me as if to say, 'What the fuck is B doing?' I'm sure they thought I was taking the piss. Soon after, we made it 3-0, and Martin Allen told me to go down and do the same thing again. That time, I really did take the piss, and just stood there waving my arms about for a few minutes. The whole thing was like a comedy sketch. That was Martin Allen in a nutshell.

Bizarrely, just when we were turning the corner and starting to win games, he was sacked. His son Charlie (Notts County, Margate) was at the club at the same time. He was a nice guy and a decent player, but suffered from the whole 'he's only playing because he's the manager's son' thing. They'd been at Notts County together too. I took him under my wing as much as I could, and before Martin Allen left, he came to me and thanked me for what I'd done for his boy. That was a nice touch. After the Gills, Allen went on to manage Barnet for the fourth time. He got them promoted from the Conference to League Two, and was doing well there – right up to the time when he requested to leave to take over at Conference side Eastleigh, who sacked him after only fourteen games. You see? Mad as a brush.

Peter Taylor, who'd been in charge at the Gills in the 1999–2000 season when he got them promoted and into the quarter-finals of the FA Cup, was the man tasked with replacing Martin Allen. He was a completely different character. He's very quiet, and strikes you as being quite shrewd. In contrast to Allen, who was all over the place, Taylor is very measured and plays his cards close to his chest. When he came to the club, it was a very tight-knit changing room, and this might have contributed to the 'us and them' situation that soon developed. He's had a long career, and by then had reached the stage where I felt he was slightly jaded and bitter toward players. In some respects he had tunnel vision, and didn't want to deviate from what he knew. For example, he used to make us train against mannequins. There's nothing wrong with that in principle, if it's incorporated into a decent training regime. But you always look great against mannequins because they obviously don't move. Under Taylor we started slow almost every game, and there'd always be an inquest afterwards. To most of the players, it was obvious. We spent so much time training against mannequins that, when we faced actual moving players, it took us a while to adjust.

Taylor had a difficult time right from the start. Things weren't going well on the field and the fans were getting on his back. A member of his family tweeted something along the lines of, 'He inherited a Conference team, so I don't know why the fans are booing him.' That was disrespectful to both the players and the fans, and did nothing at all to help Taylor.

During team meetings leading up to a fixture, most managers I have played for would discuss what the opposition was good at and how we would combat it. If our plan didn't work, you could argue that while we spent all that time trying to figure out how to stop them playing, we should have been more focused on what we were going to do, and let them worry about us. There are always going to be times when you have to adapt to set-pieces and the like, but most players think the onus should be more on the team they are playing for. You can exercise more control that way. In theory, anyway. If, for example, we play 4-4-2, and we're up against a team that plays 3-4-3, the manager might change our system to try to match the other team man for man. But because they are more used to that system than we are, they'll probably end up winning the game. So why are we changing? Why not focus on what we do best and let the opposition change for us? Because there is so much pressure on managers now, a lot of them are quick to claim the credit when their team wins, and even quicker to blame individual players, or even whole teams, when they lose. Even though they make all the important decisions, it's like they are afraid to take responsibility for them. It's a worrying trend.

The rest of that season was tough, and we eventually finished down in seventeenth place. I got into double figures in the goalscoring charts again, despite Peter Taylor's refusal to play me two games back-to-back. For some reason he had it in his head that I couldn't play two games in a week and that was that. There was no swaying him. It didn't even matter how well I played. If I scored in a game, I'd still be benched for the next one. When the season finished he broke up the changing room and got rid of a lot of players. In fairness, he did offer me a new contract but I wasn't interested. Too much had happened. At the beginning of the next season the team struggled again and at the end of December Taylor was sacked.

By this time, the #BeastModeOn thing was really starting to take off, and my profile was rising as a consequence. I was doing more and more interviews in the press and making more and more TV appearances. I started getting invited to go on *Soccer AM* on Sky Sports, which helped me reach a whole new demographic. Their audience was probably the slightly older football fan who hadn't seen any of my YouTube videos and didn't play the *FIFA* games. They initially had me on as a guest when I was at Northampton, just prior to the play-off final. It meant I had to miss a training session and had to have my absence approved by Aidy Boothroyd. I could tell he wasn't happy about it, but what could he do? It was probably one of the reasons he didn't like me. Later, I went on with Rizzle Kicks, and had to hold a shopping basket with more stuff in it than theirs. I forgot we were on live TV and swore. That wasn't my finest moment.

The YouTube stuff I did probably boosted my profile quicker than *Soccer AM* did. When I started doing videos with KSI and other YouTubers, we had the perfect mutually-beneficial relationship. They were getting a video with a reasonably high-profile footballer to boost their viewing numbers, and I was getting introduced to more people all the time. But YouTube was, and still is to an extent, a young person's medium. It's very niche, while things like *Soccer AM* are much more mainstream. To cover all bases, I need to nurture a relationship with both mediums.

All the TV stuff came naturally to me, and suited my personality down to the ground. I was never nervous. By the time I rejoined the Gills I was being regularly featured in *Nuts* and *Loaded* magazines, and then the *Sun* newspaper, which has a readership of over three million a day, did a piece on me. All of a sudden, I was getting all this media attention. That was when I first started to realise that the tide was changing. I wasn't just a footballer any more, I'd transcended that label. I was now something more than that. A sports personality. It wasn't something I planned, just as I hadn't planned the Beast Mode thing to take off the way it did, but I was immensely grateful for both avenues as they represented opportunities. A footballer's career is very short. The lucky ones get to play until their mid-thirties, perhaps playing semi-pro a while longer if they are prepared to accept less and less money as they drop down the leagues. After that it's all over, and we need to look at other ways we can generate income and put food on the table. I know I can't play forever, and I'm incredibly appreciative of the fact that I have these additional revenue streams to nurture as my career winds down. Most footballers aren't as lucky.

Northampton Town is still the club I call home. They've been good to me. So when they were hit with a winding-up order over unpaid taxes in October 2015 I was eager to do all I could to help. I auctioned off the shirt I was wearing when I scored my first hat-trick back in 2012. It was actually auctioned twice. The first time, the bidding went up to £7,500 but the guy who made the winning bid couldn't pay it. I don't think he ever thought he'd actually win. So it had to be auctioned again. Second time around it only brought in £440 and it was about four sizes too big for the guy, but at least he had the money to pay for it!

9 THE DON

AFC Wimbledon (2014–16)

The main reason I went to AFC Wimbledon in League Two was the gaffer, Neil Ardley. I'd met him the season before, after I left Northampton the second time, and he was saying all the right things to me. I didn't sign for him then only because I wanted to play in League One, and Gillingham offered me that. I could tell how much he wanted to sign me when I became a free agent again because he even agreed to meet me in Nando's. He explained that the club had a small budget, their Kingsmeadow stadium held less than 5,000, and that the only thing the club could really sell was him. To be honest, I was greatly impressed with him as a manager. He was very much the new breed, and quite innovative in his methods. Whether the team was doing good, bad or indifferently, we always got Mondays off because he believed recovery was just as important as maintaining good fitness levels. Even better, if there was no midweek game, senior players always got Wednesdays off too. I was more than happy with that, so I signed for a year with another year's option, which could be triggered if I hit certain goal and appearance targets.

I didn't know much about AFC Wimbledon as a club. I knew a few players, who had connections there. Danny Kedwell, who I got close to when I was at Gillingham, had played for them when they were in the Conference, and Barry Fuller, who I also knew from Gillingham, was there the same time as me. They all said the place was cool, but I didn't know much about the history of the club. They'd only been formed in 2002 as a direct reaction by disgruntled fans who felt betrayed by the decision by an independent commission appointed by the Football League to relocate the original Wimbledon FC to Milton Keynes and change their name to MK Dons. Considering the short time they'd been in existence, AFC Wimbledon had enjoyed a meteoric rise, starting off in the Combined Counties League (in the ninth tier of the football pyramid) and being promoted five times in nine years.

Two things I found out very quickly were that the club was extremely well run, and the fans were mad passionate. Some of the most dedicated I'd ever seen. Not only did they have a large hardcore support – even playing non-league they were regularly drawing crowds of 4,000-plus – but they are one of those clubs everyone has a soft spot for. I remember thinking to myself, this is a different kind of club, and I'm a different kind of player. We just clicked immediately, the old-school, 'Crazy Gang' ethos that remains from the 1980s when the club was still Wimbledon FC, and me, the strongest player on *FIFA*. Akinfenwa and AFC Wimbledon could have been made for each other. The media guy at the club told me that after I joined they had more interview requests for me than any other player they'd ever had. It was a level they weren't really used to. National newspapers weren't in the habit of contacting AFC Wimbledon for player interviews until I signed for them.

We played Chelsea in pre-season. Back when John Terry was involved in that race storm with Anton Ferdinand, some member of the press asked me what I would do if I ever came up against John Terry on the pitch. I can't remember my exact words, but it all got twisted into AKINFENWA WANTS TO SMASH JOHN TERRY! Obviously, a while later this game came up and we finally met face-to-face. He gets lot of bad press. Being England captain, everything he did was analysed and magnified. But, to be fair, Terry is a cool guy. He said that if we clashed during the game and he ended up on the floor, the media would have a field day with it, so we both agreed to just stay away from each other.

I saw straightaway what a great manager Neil Ardley was. His tactics were spot-on that day. We would let Chelsea have the ball in their own half, but then as soon as they reached the halfway line, we would start pressing them all over the pitch giving them no space and no time on the ball. It worked like a treat. It was a strong Chelsea team, but after an hour we were 2-0 up. The gaffer had told us before the game that after the hour mark he'd start making substitutions, so the game got broken up, we lost some focus, and ended up losing 3-2. Terry scored a brace late on. Who else?

That first season, Ardley pretty much let me be me on the pitch. I never consider myself a luxury player. I'm always willing to get stuck in. But I'm usually the focal point of a team, and if I'm not on it, it's very easy for me to become a passenger. It's something I've been especially wary of since I broke my leg and my mobility took a hit. Now, before every match, I tell myself I have to be on my game because if not, I'm just there and the team is carrying me. I hate that feeling. Everyone knows I'm not the kind of player to cover every blade of grass chasing down loose balls. Look at me. I just can't do that shit. But people know exactly what they're going to get with me. If there is a pair of big hulking centre-halves on the opposing team, I'll be the one taking the fight right to them and trying to smash holes through them.

As I did with almost every manager I've played under, when I first met Ardley I told him there might be ten games in a season where I would pretty much be non-effective. His response was one I'd never heard before. He said, 'That's fine. I understand. But I want you to understand that it's my job to try and get that ten down to five.' I appreciated that. Even when he reaches the twilight of his career, every player wants to grow and improve. Something else that sticks in my mind from when I signed is the strength of the changing room. If you have a good changing room, it runs itself, and one of the best I ever had was at AFC Wimbledon. We had a good mix of solid, dependable pros and young, hungry talent.

Something I wasn't prepared for was the sheer hatred the AFC Wimbledon fans have for MK Dons. I talked before about the rivalry between Swansea and Cardiff. This is right up there, if not above it. It was so bad that when we pulled them in the first round of the Football League Cup at the start of the 2014–15 season, the fans refused to go to the game and boycotted it. It was such a weird reaction. In the run-up, all we kept hearing about was this seventeen-year-old called Dele Alli (Tottenham Hotspur and England) who was running games for the Dons. During the match he tackled me, hard. I told him to ease up, and he turned around and told me to shut my mouth! I decided to chase him, to try to get close enough to shoulder-barge him or something, but I couldn't get within ten feet of him. I told him I was going to punch him up, and he was just like, 'Yeah? Come on, then!' He wasn't even bothered, there wasn't so much as a trace of fear in his eyes. I just thought, 'Fuck it, I'll see him in the tunnel at half-time. This kid needs to be taught a lesson.' It's not unusual to trade insults or for players to get under each other other's skin on the pitch. Things can get emotional out there. I had issues with Guy Branston before, and Tommy Mooney when he was at Walsall. How I deal with it is to tell them we'll sort it out at half-time, away from the cameras and the officials. That way there'll be no repercussions. Nobody throws punches on the pitch.

So the interval came, and I raced into the tunnel to wait for young Master Alli. Next thing I know all the players on both teams were in between us, trying to keep me away from him, and he's walking past still smirking at me! I was thinking, 'Who is this brazen little kid who has no respect?' If I'd got my hands on him, I'd have broken Alli in half that day. No shadow of a doubt. He really wound me up. Luckily for him, and England, his manager at the time, Karl Robinson, a guy I have a lot of respect for, talked me down and I let it go. They beat us 3-1, but even though we lost, it was one of my best games for the club. I won a lot of friends that day. Just not Dele Alli! It's all cool now. I see him at EA events and it's all in the past.

Ardley is a great man manager. I remember him telling me that he always knew I was good, but he just didn't appreciate how good I was, until he saw me play. That being said, I didn't score until my tenth game in all competitions. That's probably the longest I've ever gone, certainly at a new club. I told the gaffer when I scored my first goal for the club I was going to run down the touchline and hug him. He had to wait a while for that hug! I finally scored in a 3-0 home win over Burton Albion, then I scored again in the same match, and I got the winner a couple of days later against Morecambe. You often find that when you break your duck, the goals will flow. I struck up a decent partnership with Matt Tubbs (Crawley Town, Portsmouth), who we had on loan from Bournemouth, but even so, the team struggled a bit. We were still trying to figure out how to play to our strengths, as often happens when a team is trying to incorporate new players.

Not long after I started scoring, we played MK Dons again, this time in the second round of the Football League Trophy.

Lucky for him, and us, probably, Dele Alli didn't play in that one. Before the game, the gaffer told us he wanted to play a team to run the opposition down, so me, Tubbs and Sean Rigg (Bristol Rovers, Port Vale) all started on the bench. The idea was that we would come on and do the damage late on. At half-time we were 2-1 down, the gaffer put us on, and me and Rigg both scored to grab a 3-2 win. I think that was the first time we'd ever beaten them, and the elation we felt from the fans was like nothing else I've ever experienced. It meant everything to them. For me, as a player, it felt amazing to be part of that legacy. Until then, I knew MK Dons were the enemy because of the history between the two clubs, which had obviously led to a huge rivalry. But I hadn't been there long, so to me they were just another team. Ardley told me afterwards that was one of the most satisfying wins he'd ever had. To come up with a plan, see it through, and have it pay dividends at the end must be the ultimate reward for a manager.

After beating York City in the first round of the FA Cup, we played Wycombe Wanderers in the second. They'd already beaten us 2-0 at their place in the league, and I sensed the gaffer wanted us to do well in this game. He had us training at 100 mph. I couldn't breathe! Everyone in football knows that when I'm tired, I'm at my most irritable. When I'm struggling to breathe, don't fuck with me. I have a saying, 'There's no shame in the game staying in your football lane.' So that's what I do. I stay in my lane. We'd never trained like that for anyone else. So, in front of the whole team, I asked Ardley what he thought he was doing running us that hard. He said, 'If we train at this intensity, when we come to play the game, it won't be this hard and it will increase our chances of getting a result.' The funny thing was, he was right. We won 1-0 and got through to the third round. Amazing.

One of the club investors then told us that if we drew a top-four club at their place in the third round, he would take the whole team to Las Vegas. Obviously who we got in the draw was out of our hands, but that was a great incentive. I was at home when the draw was made, watching it on Sky Sports, not fully paying attention, nor realising the magnitude of everything. When the balls came out they paired us up with Liverpool, my boyhood team. After a few more draws were made, it dawned on me. We were playing Liverpool! The only sour point was that we'd been drawn as the home team and they'd be coming to Kingsmeadow. While that obviously has its advantages, Premier League grounds are generally much bigger than League Two grounds, which means more gate receipts. Plus, I really wanted that trip to Las Vegas.

I was popular at AFC Wimbledon, and by then had made

a name for myself beyond that as something of a media personality with the *FIFA* and Beast Mode stuff, but the Liverpool game took my popularity to a whole new level. People often wonder about footballers having divided loyalties at clubs. I'd been a Liverpool supporter all my life, and spent my whole life in football. This was the first time in my career I'd be playing against them. I can't speak for anyone else, but for me, that was the only time I've ever wanted Liverpool to lose.

Up until then, I'd played almost every game of the season for AFC Wimbledon, but then I got a slight Achilles injury and it was touch-and-go whether I'd be fit enough. I remember telling the gaffer that even if I had to hobble onto the pitch on one leg, I was playing. I also told my teammates that I wanted Steven Gerrard's shirt, and if any of them tried sneaking in there before me, I was going to punch them up on sight. Just to make sure there would be no misunderstandings, I called up Joe Allen (Liverpool, Stoke City and Wales), who I knew from my Swansea days, and told him to tell Gerrard not to give it to anyone else. It was a weird little role-reversal, because over the past couple of seasons, most of the players I go up against ask for my shirt. It's an honour. But of course, you can only give it to one person and at the smaller clubs it's not like you can go around giving shirts away willy-nilly. We usually only get given two kits a season. So if you give yours away, you have to buy yourself another one.

The media attention in the build-up was insane. We were massive underdogs, so we had nothing to lose. The whole thing was kind of geared towards recreating the famous FA Cup final from 1988 when the old Wimbledon Crazy Gang beat Liverpool at Wembley against all the odds. Henry Winter from the *Telegraph* interviewed me, and remarked on how passionate I was about football. I told him I'm not just passionate about football, I'm passionate about life. I play with a smile. I was asked what it was like playing my boyhood heroes. I replied that it was either play for them or play against them, and it was probably safe to say it wasn't going to be the former any time soon. I've never been under any illusions about that!

I had complete faith in Ardley's tactics. When we'd played Liverpool's Premier League rivals Chelsea in pre-season he got it spot on, and there were a lot of similarities in the way the two teams played. Before the game, the gaffer asked us if we wanted to stay in a hotel the night before. The players all said no. We wanted to keep it as close as possible to a normal match day. I remember lining up against Liverpool and noticing how strong they all looked. Emre Can (Bayern Munich, Bayer

Leverkusen and Germany), Mamadou Sakho (Paris Saint-Germain and France), Jordan Henderson (Sunderland and England). They are BIG guys. Tall and muscular with it. When the game kicked off I was in my element. The first ball that came up to me, I just ran at Martin Škrtel (Zenit Saint Petersburg, Fenerbahçe and Slovakia) and put the fear of God into him. I thought, 'Even if he wins the ball, he's going to know he's in a game.'

Liverpool were having an indifferent season. It was our game plan to try to bring them down to our level and make them play League Two football. Our fans helped enormously with that. It's a cliché, but the fans are very often the twelfth man. It's true. They inspire a team. That day, they were on the job, and created an amazing atmosphere. Probably one of the best I've ever played in. The difference between us and them was Gerrard. He was almost thirty-five at the time, and playing out his last season at Liverpool, but he was a class above in everything he did. He was so precise. Twelve minutes gone, he drifted in the way he does and banged in a superb header to make it 1-0. We had no choice then but to ramp up the intensity and go after them. It was the FA Cup, where fairytales come true and anything could happen. The ref kept blowing up against us, and I remember saying to him, 'Stop babying them! We're League Two, they're the Prem team. Give us a chance!'

And then came my moment. I still get goosebumps when I think about it now. Our midfielder George Francombe whipped in a corner and I pushed Škrtel away to get some space. At the time it was well-documented that the Liverpool goalkeeper Simon Mignolet (Sunderland and Belgium) was poor on corners, which was something we'd been looking to exploit the whole game. The ball bounced and one of our defenders got something on it. It looped up, came off the bar, dropped to the ground, and I remember thinking, 'I can poke this in!' The world seemed to slow to a standstill, a hush fell over the crowd, I gritted my teeth and I went for it. I made contact with the ball, saw it cross the line, and my next thought was, 'Shit. I just scored against Liverpool!'

The AFC Wimbledon players started jumping all over me, and I ran over to the corner where our hardcore fans would normally be sitting, not realising that this being the FA Cup, things had been moved around. So I ended up accidentally celebrating in front of the Liverpool fans. I walked away thinking, 'Why the fuck are they all swearing at me?'

Later in the game, the ball came up to me. I controlled it, and looked to pass to my right. But Philippe Coutinho (Inter Milan and Brazil) and Lucas Leiva (Grêmio, Lazio and Brazil) were both coming at me and blocked that route off. I thought I was going to lose the ball. So as a last resort I did a little pirouette and laid it off. It must have looked amazing, because the roar from the crowd was as big as when the goal went in. That's another video that went big on YouTube. We went in at half-time 1-1. The gaffer didn't even need to give us a team talk. We were buzzing. We all knew what needed to be done. We had to keep Liverpool out for forty-five minutes, and then we'd be taking trips to Anfield and Vegas. It doesn't get any better than that. It's all the incentive you need.

In the second half, up stepped Gerrard to take a free-kick, and the moment it left his boot I knew it was in. It was sublime. Even as an AFC Wimbledon player, you had to stand back and admire it. In the end the game finished 2-1, and in all honesty it could have been worse. We had no choice but to push for another equaliser in the latter stages which left us wide open to counter-attacks and we made a couple of goal-line clearances. But all in all, we gave a good account of ourselves. At the final whistle, I regressed to being a fan again and went straight over to Stevie G to get his shirt. While we were chatting, I congratulated him and told him to go on and win the cup before he left. The history books will show that they ended up going out to Aston Villa in the semis, but I did my bit!

By this time, all the rest of the AFC Wimbledon players had gone back to the changing room, and they're all watching me clapping our fans on my own on the TV. I didn't even know the camera was on me. Those pictures became iconic. I've always been popular with the fans of whatever club I played for. But for me, that moment was the start of me being known internationally. I also believe that us losing so gallantly also won us some favour in the football world. We were the plucky underdogs who had given everything, only to go down to one of the giants of British football. It was what everyone expected, but maybe most people expected us to lose by a few more goals.

Immediately after the game, Liverpool TV interviewed me and I think it got four or five million hits. I took a selfie with Mario Balotelli (AC Milan, Manchester City and Italy), and he posted it on his Instagram account. It meant a lot that so many of the players took the time to interact and have conversations with me, instead of just saying 'Good game', and walking off. They talked to me as an equal. It felt like every media outlet in the country wanted some quotes, and I was definitely the last one to leave the ground that day. I still find it crazy that there were all these millionaire footballers wandering around yet all the attention, all the focus, was on me.

Before the Liverpool game, I'd been trying to get verified on Twitter. I had 40 or 50,000 followers. But they were saying

I didn't play at a high enough level. I don't know what difference that makes, but there you go. You can't argue with Twitter. Afterwards, I got about 40,000 tweets with my name in, and the very next day Twitter verified me. Until then, the biggest celebs I'd had on my phone were Ian Wright (Arsenal and England) and Louis from One Direction. Afterwards, I was chatting to Balotelli and Robbie Fowler (Liverpool, Manchester City and England), and Stevie G was commenting on my tweets. I was like, 'What's going on?' Not long afterwards, I was invited to an NBA game at Wembley. I was rubbing shoulders not only with the basketball elite, but also with people like Eden Hazard (Chelsea and Belgium), Didier Drogba (Chelsea, Marseille and Ivory Coast) and Thierry Henry (Arsenal, Barcelona and France). He actually told me he'd been watching me, and commented on what a good season I was having. Incredible. Just the fact that he knew who I was blew me away. It took me an hour to get off the court because so many people were asking me for my picture. It was insane.

The Liverpool game turned out to be Matt Tubbs's last for us. He had his loan terminated when Portsmouth went in for him on a permanent deal. Consequently, we found it harder to find the net in the second half of the season and started slipping down the league. We played Mansfield at home, and my leg got smashed by one of their defenders, Luke Waterfall (Lincoln City, Wrexham), who they had in on loan from Scunthorpe. It was the same one I'd broken. I honestly thought I'd broken it again. Until then I'd been wearing these special protective shin pads I'd got at Northampton, which covered the whole section, but I'd only recently stopped wearing them because I didn't think I needed them any more. I had to go off, and we lost the game 1-0. About forty-five minutes after the game finished when I was at home wondering whether my leg was broken again, someone showed me this Mansfield centre-half's Snapchat. He'd posted a picture of himself with the caption, 'Akinfenwa pussy came off after 5 minutes.'

I couldn't let that slide, so I rang up Abdul Osman (Partick Thistle, Crewe Alex) who I knew from my Northampton Town days, and I'd heard used to play with this guy, and he gave me his phone number. I was absolutely fuming. I can live with losing a battle. If he was saying he was stronger, faster or just better than me, then fine. But this guy was laughing at me because I'd had to go off injured! What kind of person does that? So I rang him up, probably while he was still on the coach going home, and I lost it with him. I told him when we played them at their place, the first thing I was going to do when we arrived was march into their changing room and punch him in his face.

I didn't give a fuck. The guy tried to apologise, and even followed me on Twitter to do it, but I wasn't having any of it. So time marched on and a couple of days before we played up at Mansfield, all the guys were asking whether I was still going to punch this guy, but by then his loan had finished and I didn't see him again.

We finished in fifteenth place, with Tubbsy and I scoring fifteen goals apiece in all competitions. I was so used to only playing an hour at Gillingham that, for the first half of the season, when the clock crept toward the hour mark, I'd keep looking over to the touchline, expecting to see my number being held up. It hardly ever was. That season I played in almost every game, and was very rarely substituted. For me it was a beautiful thing, because it completely dispelled Peter Taylor's myth that I couldn't play two games in a row. Personally, that season was a triumph for me. I finished joint top scorer, played and scored against my boyhood team, and won both the Players' Player of the Season and Supporters' Player of the Season awards.

My profile increased to such an extent that in the summer I was considering going to play in the MLS in America. It would have been the ideal chance to get the Beast Mode name out there. But at the time, Mich was pregnant with my youngest so it didn't make a lot of sense to do that. A lot of League Two clubs wanted me, but I told Neil Ardley that if I was staying in England I'd sign with AFC Wimbledon again because of how much I'd enjoyed my time there. After I signed, the gaffer said to me, 'I'm so glad you stayed. I didn't want people to think I couldn't keep my star players.'

• • •

At the time, it was all going so well with Neil Ardley and AFC Wimbledon. I don't think anyone could have foreseen how it would all end. In the summer the club signed two other strikers, Tom Elliott (Leeds United, Stockport County, Cambridge United) and Lyle Taylor (Bournemouth, Sheffield United, Scunthorpe United). The gaffer told me that on too many occasions we had been nullified by the opposition due to our style of play, so he needed more options up front, which was probably true. Elliott was supposed to be the main man, and he deserved to be. In the old-fashioned big man–small man strike partnership, he can play both roles. He can hold the ball up, and he can make darting runs. It was Taylor who caught the eye, though. He went on to grab twenty-plus goals that season.

Even if we played a 4-4-2 formation, three into two doesn't go, so I knew my chances would probably be limited. Being challenged has always brought the best out in me. I was happy to play a full game, or an hour, or half an hour, whatever it took to help the team out. It doesn't always have to be about me, as long as I'm contributing. At my age, I'm not running away from anybody but there was no other player like me at the club, and I still had the ability to change games. Even so, the gaffer pulled me aside one day in the first half of the season and said he didn't think I was the same player I had been the season before. I think it was partly because I was on such a pedestal the first season. I had to take a lot of weight on my shoulders in certain departments because for much of the time there was just nobody else. After Tubbsy left, me and Ade Azeez were the only strikers at the club, and Ade was still a bit young and raw.

A turning point came when Stevenage beat us at home 2-1 just before Christmas. We'd arranged a train to Manchester immediately after the game for our Christmas party, and didn't even have time to do the Man of the Match or anything. That got us a lot of stick from the fans who were saying all we wanted to do was party and we didn't care about the result. It wasn't a good situation, so the gaffer told me to keep an eye on everyone and keep things in check. We'd all bought matching Christmas tracksuits just for a laugh, and I posted a photo of us on Instagram to show how together we were as a team.

Later, Ardley said he wouldn't have done that because in his mind it was sending the wrong message. I think our relationship started to disintegrate from that point.

We played Cambridge away after Christmas, and though we won 4-1 and it was one of my best games of the season, I remember telling Ardley I wasn't actually that happy at AFC Wimbledon any more. He looked at me and said, 'I know. I can see it.' Elliott and Taylor had formed a formidable partnership by then, and I was being slowly phased out. I started getting the feeling that the gaffer was doing all he could to prove he didn't need me, and could succeed without me. I don't ever want to say that my profile is so big it causes problems, but I think that was basically what it was. I started feeling sorry for myself, and he wasn't prepared to help me snap out of it. Everyone needs a pep talk every now and again, even if it's just a bit of reassurance, but he was happy to just let me wallow in self-pity, which wasn't doing anyone any good. By then I'd got to my bitching stage, so I wasn't exactly a pleasure to be around. All players have bad patches and, for the good of the club, it's the manager's job to help them snap out of it. Confidence is a fragile thing. But when I had a bad patch, the gaffer just said, 'Right, you're done.'

Maybe he was right. Maybe I wasn't doing enough for the team. I've always said it's okay for managers to criticise me. If you don't think I'm doing enough as a player, that's your prerogative as a manager and you're well within your rights to say so. Come and talk to me about it. I'm not going to bite your head off. I might argue my point, but I'll be reasonable. More often than not, I'll know if I'm in the wrong, and I'll hold my hands up and admit as much. I explained to the gaffer that I was trying to find my form again and that it might take me a couple of games. I was pretty much asking for a bit of slack. I played the game after Cambridge, which was Mansfield at home. We won, but Ardley pulled me off after half-time and I hardly got into the team again. I remember telling him I'm not the kind of player who can get things done in ten or fifteen minutes off the bench. I need time to get going. And if I'm only getting a few minutes here and there, by the time I get into the game, it's over.

That month, Eastleigh came in for me with a ridiculous offer for a Conference team. Way more money than I was on at AFC Wimbledon. They'd done the same thing the previous January. On that occasion, Ardley refused their offer then called me to give me a heads-up. This time, he called me and asked whether I wanted to stay or not. That spoke volumes to me. He was obviously more than willing to let me go. The only reason I turned down Eastleigh was that I didn't want to drop out of the league. I had no animosity toward Ardley. We're still cool now. But I do feel that if he'd had his way I would've been gone.

Because I'm such a big character and have a lot of influence in the changing room, if I'm not in their immediate plans I know managers will be looking over their shoulder thinking, 'Shit, what's B saying about me?' That is one of those instances when being such a big character has an adverse effect. The gaffer would go out of his way to tell me it was for the good of the team, but I always felt that he was going out of his way to stamp his authority.

Not long after that, the gaffer sent me on for the last couple of minutes of a game and it was obvious to all that I didn't want to be there. That was the first time in over fifteen years as a professional that I've ever gone on the pitch with the mindset that I wasn't going to give 100 per cent. I just wasn't in the right frame of mind. I was too unsettled. Ardley rang me up afterwards and chewed me out over the phone saying I'd let myself, him, the fans and the club down. I was thinking, 'Well, you've created this situation. What did you expect would happen?' That made me think beyond doubt that I was done with the club. It would be best all round if I left.

Lyle Taylor was knocking in goals for fun at the time. I used to give him a pep talk: 'Lyle, go walk on water.' That's how good he is. He's a very good footballer, but to me he has the personality to act like a bit of an infant. And a very sharp tongue to go with it. I feel he aggravates people. Me, I'm very respectful. I won't banter anyone unless they banter me first. He thought he was the main man, and would say things to the other players along the lines of, 'B will do whatever I tell him to do.' Like I was a puppy or something. He was getting most of the goals, and it seemed to me like he wanted to project that alpha-male image to the rest of the team. For most of the season, I let it go. I just let him be Lyle to get the best out of him on the pitch. Other people warned him about me, but it didn't seem to faze him at all. It got to the point where I had to have a word: I told him that if I wasn't in the room, don't be saying my name. I don't want to hear it. We were in the changing room before a game one day when he turned to me and said, 'I'm going to start body-slamming people.'

He was referring to me.

I totally lost it. I pushed him into the corner and started laying into him with some firm punches, just to show him who the main man really was. I started on his legs, and worked my way up his body while he did his best to cover up. Don't get me wrong, Lyle is a cool person away from football, but he likes to cross lines and test people. That's his thing. So everybody wanted to see this beat-down. If Barry Fuller hadn't intervened, it would have got really proper nasty because he wasn't taking it well. Barry Fuller, my former teammate at Gillingham, is another player I class as a friend. His most admirable quality is his determination. He battled back from a career-threatening injury, and is one of the most inspirational people I know. When he talks, people listen. He's also great at calming people down. If he hadn't been there that day, Lyle would have been in trouble. It's very unlike me to do that before a game, but on this occasion I was pushed too far.

There's a lot of testosterone at a football club, and sometimes action needs to be taken so throughout my career when I give beat-downs I've developed a level system. The higher the level, the harder I go at them. Because I'm right-handed, level one is a left-hand punch. Level two is a right-hander. Level three is a combo. There are a few players walking around who can say they've taken me to level four: Myles Weston, Antonio German, Harry Pell. Lyle Taylor is the first to push me all the way to level five. I unleashed! I just didn't go for his face. It's mostly playful, but it does get serious on occasion and that was borderline. After that we didn't talk for a few days, and then I got called to the gaffer's office. I went in and Lyle is sitting there looking glum. Ardley says, 'Why didn't I know about what happened with you and Lyle?'

I thought, 'Really? This is what it's come to?' It was like being back at school and being called into the headmaster's office for a telling-off. He said Lyle wanted to sort things out but because I wasn't speaking to him, this was the only way he could do it. It all blew over pretty fast. What happened needed to happen, and we were both all the better for it afterwards.

I still wasn't getting game time, so just as the loan window was closing in March, Ardley finally agreed to let me go. Dean agreed a deal with Crawley Town, and to be honest I was looking forward to leaving. I'd been speaking to one of the players there, and he said it was cool. Crawley was a small club with no expectations. I could just go there and enjoy my football again. But just before the move, I went on as sub at Bristol Rovers and got sent off. I had a falling-out with the ref in that one. One of the Bristol players was pulling my shirt, and the ref gave a free-kick against me. He thought I was complaining that he was only penalising me because I was black, but I was actually trying to tell him they were pushing me in the back. He wasn't having any of it and sent me off in injury time for dissent. Neil Ardley told me the club weren't going to appeal the ban because the ref was adamant that the red card was justified and we'd probably lose the appeal, so that put paid to the Crawley deal. They needed someone right then, and didn't want to hang around while I served my ban.

As I was sitting out the two-game ban, I'd still go to the

games and drive in to training. One day, as I pulled into the ground, I looked in the mirror and saw my own face change. I had an epiphany. It suddenly occurred to me that it takes a lot of energy to be miserable. Fuck that. Whatever happened, whether I was playing or not, I was there until the end of the season and me moping around wasn't doing anyone any favours, least of all me. From that day, I resolved to make the most of what was sure to be my last couple of months at a great club.

In March and April, we went on a mad run and won six out of seven games. We were 1-1 at Plymouth, and the gaffer sent me on for a cameo at the end. I ended up scoring the winner, and in that instant my mojo came back. I started enjoying my football again. We sneaked into the play-offs, and all I was thinking was that if I get playing time, I was going to cause teams problems. I had a point to prove, but, more importantly, I was feeling good about myself again.

The last game of the season at home was against Newport County. With our play-off place guaranteed, the gaffer rested the first team and played mostly youth and fringe players. I played up front with an eighteen-year-old called Toyosi Olusanya, who was making his debut. I was just on another level that day. I remember telling myself to never go back in my shell again, and to keep a smile on my face whatever happened. It was 0-0 going into the last ten minutes when Olusanya went down in the box and the ref awarded us a pen. Earlier in the season, Callum Kennedy had lost his father, and he told me that next time he scored he was going to dedicate the goal to his dad. The designated penalty-taker at the club was Lyle Taylor. The second penalty-taker was George Francomb, so the chances of me being involved in any penalty kicks anyway were pretty remote. But that last game, neither Lyle nor George were playing, so the onus was on me. I got my hands on the ball and was stepping up, when Callum came up and asked if he could take it. I told him it was Olusanya's debut, and because he'd won the pen in the first place, he should take it. It would mean a lot to the kid, and give him the kind of confidence boost which would only benefit the club going forward. Callum wasn't happy about it, but reluctantly agreed. To appease him a bit, I told him the next pen was his, no question. Lucky for him Olusanya took the pen, scored, and we won 1-0. Happy days. He dedicated the goal to the 'legend Akinfenwa', which was nice.

In training afterwards, Callum came up to me and told me he was taking the next pen. I explained that football worked in hierarchies. That's how it's always been. We had designated pen-takers one and two, and after that, the next most experienced person on the pitch gets the choice, preferably a striker.

That was me. And unless I said otherwise, I'd be taking the penalty. Apart from the personal standpoint, it made sense for the team because that would give us the best chance of scoring, rather than put all the pressure on a defender who's probably only been in the penalty area three times in the whole season. However, knowing the situation with his dad, I agreed to let him have it. Like I said, I wasn't even the designated penalty-taker so the chances of me being involved in any penalty drama at that time were pretty remote.

As soon as I knew we were playing Accrington Stanley in the play-off semis, I knew we'd get to the final. In the league, we'd drawn with them at home and beaten them away. They were a good team going forward, but I knew we could bully them. In the first leg we were drawing 0-0 at home, and needed a goal. The gaffer sent me on, and I immediately hit the post. Then, in injury time, I set up Tom Beere for the winner. We'd developed an interesting habit of scoring late goals that season and that was another welcome addition. There's a picture of Tom and me celebrating the goal. The feeling when the ball crossed the line was more than relief. It was a huge outpouring of emotion. I kept telling myself that this is the power positive energy has.

When I wasn't picked to start the second leg, I wasn't even disappointed. By then, I'd adopted the 'whatever will be will be' ethos. I'd been through the worst, and I flat-out refused to feel sorry for myself. At half-time in the second leg, we were a goal down, and the gaffer sent me on again. Even when they scored their second, I still knew we were going to win the tie. There wasn't a shadow of a doubt in my mind. I scored a header to take us level on aggregate. The match went to extra-time, Lyle Taylor scored to put us in front, and then the floodlights went off. There was talk of us having to replay the fixture. I was like, 'Nah. It's not going to happen. I won't allow it. There's no way they're taking this away from us.' The lights came back on after about ten minutes, so there was no massive drama. After the game, somebody asked me what I thought when the lights went off. I said, 'Mate, I was raised in Hackney. We played football in the dark all the time.' That quote went big on social media. When I said it, I wasn't even thinking in soundbites, I was just being myself.

The same guy who was going to take us to Vegas for playing a top-four team away in the FA Cup made the same offer for getting to the play-offs. So in my head I was thinking, 'We can go out and win the final, celebrate, go to sleep, then wake up and fly to Vegas.' You can't have a better couple of days than that. A couple of days before the game, which was an even bigger event in the club's history than the Liverpool game, Ardley called me into his office. He told me he didn't want it made public, as it would distract the team, but he wouldn't be offering me a new contract. I said it was cool, I knew that way back in January. There could be no better way to go out than with promotion. I wanted to go out with a bang, and do something unforgettable for the fans. Somehow, it got out anyway. I don't know how, it didn't come from me, but Sky broke the news that the final was to be my last game for AFC Wimbledon.

In the play-off final against Plymouth Argyle, I again felt that Ardley didn't want to make it about me so he was keen to downplay the fact I was even there. I was sitting on the bench thinking, 'Unleash me!' His first substitution had me scratching my head. He sent on Jonathan Meades who, to be fair, had played the whole season, got injured late on, and fought to be back for the final. I'm not knocking the decision to play him. But he normally plays left-back, and the thing was, Callum Kennedy was filling in there and doing well, so the gaffer took off a midfielder and Meades went in there. I wouldn't have made that move but I'm not the manager am I?

When I finally went on as sub it was goalless with 77 minutes played. The game was going nowhere, and was there to be won. So Neil Ardley sent me on, begrudgingly I think, to change things up. Within a minute we'd scored through Lyle Taylor, who then went off, and then deep in injury time Adebayo Azeez was fouled in the box. It was then I realised that just like when we played Newport, neither of our designated penalty takers were on the field. Fresh from the conversations we'd had in training after the Newport game, Callum Kennedy strolled up fully expecting to take the pen. I know I'd said he could take the next one that came along. But when I'd told him that, I didn't know the next one to come along would be in the play-off final! I was just thinking it was my last game for AFC Wimbledon. What better way to say goodbye than with the winning penalty in the play-off final?

I said to Callum, 'I need to take this pen.' And what got my back up was the fact that he was blanking me and pretending not to hear what I was saying. He was just being belligerent. I was still trying not to make a scene, which is difficult in such a big game at Wembley in front of nearly 60,000 people, but there was no way in the world I was letting anyone else take that penalty. There's slightly more to the story. He'd also been told he was leaving, so it was his last game, too. And then there was the fact he'd been trying to score for his dad. But I'd been doing all I could to make that happen for him. He'd even taken a couple of free-kicks in recent matches which really should have been taken by others. The other thing coming into play, the final piece of the jigsaw, was my penalty miss for Swansea ten years earlier. In my head I was thinking if I could knock this one in, I could somehow make it right. It was almost as if life had come full circle, taking me to that one moment and offering me the chance to redeem myself and lay the ghosts to rest.

But Callum wouldn't let go of the ball. We must have been arguing for a good minute or so. What helped things along was a Plymouth defender coming over and knocking the ball out of his hand. It saved me doing it. I remember another Plymouth player trying to throw me off by telling me I was going to miss. But I just told him even if I missed, it didn't matter. We were already 1-0 up. The game was effectively over. It was a shot to nothing. I put the ball down and slotted it into the net. I'm not usually nervous taking penalties, but I did have a few twinges before that one. It was a great feeling to leave on a high, and give the gaffer a parting shot, too. To his credit, when it went in Callum came running up and said, 'You're a bastard, but I love you! You're just bigger than me.'

I hardly ever do this, especially as some referees are very quick on the draw with those yellow cards, but when the goal went in the first thing I did was rip off my shirt to reveal my blue Beast Mode undergarment. I didn't do it intentionally. I could even have got in trouble for it because you're not supposed to show any sponsors. I was just so elated. I couldn't have planned that day any better. The interview I gave just after, where I said I was unemployed and any interested managers could hit me up on WhatsApp, will probably go down in history as one of the most famous post-match interviews ever. But I didn't plan that to go the way it did, I promise you. It just happened. I'm spontaneous. Thinking about it now, maybe I should have had a 'Hit me up on WhatsApp' T-shirt made for the occasion. In any case, the response from that interview was overwhelming.

I don't know if it's true, but I later heard that when the pen went in, Ardley over on the touchline turned around with a less than ecstatic look on his face. By the time I got to hear about it I was gone, so I didn't look too closely into it. As I've said before, I've always gone out of my way to be respectful. Especially to my managers. At the end of the day, they are my bosses. Even after I leave a club, I'm always careful to call them gaffer. Except in Neil Ardley's case, where after I left I purposely called him Neil.

I don't hold any grudges. I left AFC Wimbledon after two great seasons with a smile on my face, a lot of new friends, and some fantastic memories. For me, that play-off win eclipsed even scoring against Liverpool, and is hands down the highlight of my footballing journey. There are players who spend their whole careers in the top flight and never score at Wembley. Immediately after the game we got on the bus and went back to Kingsmeadow stadium to celebrate, then, as planned, the next day we flew to Vegas.

• • •

While I was at AFC Wimbledon, I finally gave Mich the fourth child she wanted in Jaylan. Of course, by this time I already had four children, so I wasn't too keen on the idea of having another when Mich brought it up. Plus, I was coming to the end of my footballing career and had a lot to think about. But it was what I'd promised her, and what we'd always talked about. She even called the order they appeared in. Girl, boy, girl, boy. They are all outgoing and opinionated, but I love how all my kids have different traits. Being the oldest at ten, Kamira is the dominant, demanding one, while five-year-old Kaliyah is the diva. She's definitely her mother's daughter. Ajani, my eldest, is big in size but soft in attitude. I can see him being big and tough when he's older and certainly carrying on the Beast Mode ethos. Seven-year-old Jai is a proper little man's man. While the girls are all off reading, he's kicking a ball around and when I go to the gym, he wants to come with me. Out of them all, I probably spend more time with him, just because he needs it more. He's small for his age so I think he might have a touch of Little Man Syndrome. He always has something to prove and he never backs down. Jaylan, being the youngest, thinks he has the right to boss the rest of us around, and is a proper little showman. When he walks into a room, he wants everyone to know about it and he expects a round of applause every time he finishes a meal. I have a feeling out of all my kids, he might turn out to be the most troublesome. They all came to the play-off final, and to have them all there to see me score a goal was an absolute joy. Afterwards I could say, 'That's what your daddy does!'

10 ONE MORE ROUND

Wycombe Wanderers (2016–)

In the wake of the play-off final and my 'Come and get me' plea, the amount of interest I got was mind-boggling. Especially for a thirty-four-year-old who'd played sporadically and scored only eight goals in the whole season. I was fielding offers not only from all over the country, but all over the world and talked to clubs in Turkey, Australia, Kuwait, Mexico and America. It was big news. The *Daily Mirror* ran a poll asking readers to vote whether or not I should move to LA Galaxy, mainly because I'd said something jokingly about how great it would be to have

Stevie Gerrard playing behind me, and 70 per cent of readers said I should. I spoke to Dean about my next move, and in his eyes it was really simple. No matter how much money was on the table, there was no way I could move abroad at that stage in my career, and I didn't want to go up north either. My life revolves around London town. It's my home, and where all the people and things I cherish are.

When I was on holiday in Las Vegas, the Bristol Rovers manager, Darrell Clarke, approached me and said his club were interested. I probably should have known who he was, but I didn't. There are ninety-two clubs in the Football League, you'd be hard-pressed to find anyone who can name the manager of every club and pick him out of a crowd. At some point Gareth Ainsworth, the Wycombe Wanderers player/manager, texted me. I'd played against him many times down the years, and there'd always been a mutual respect between us. I remember seeing a segment about this footballer on Sky Sports once who was into punk rock and played in a band. It turned out to be him. He was all about doing things the way he wanted, rather than the way other people thought he should do them. Unorthodox people always hit the right notes with me, because I'm unorthodox myself. I respect individuals, and people with integrity.

Dean and I went to meet Ainsworth on a farm owned by the Wanderers chairman. I remember they offered me ice cream, and my first thought was that it was a test. I was thinking should I take it or not? In the end, I took the ice cream. Of course I did. It was free ice cream! I remembered the time back on the estate when the ice-cream man would come around and I didn't have enough money to buy one. There I was, all those years later, getting it free. I'd arrived! After listening to Ainsworth tell me about the club and the way he did things, I was sold.

One of the big factors in me joining Wycombe was the changing room. At AFC Wimbledon, Neil played a part but ultimately it was the changing room that got us promoted. We had such fantastic team spirit, and a desire to not just work for each other, but to go the extra mile to get the job done. What we lacked in skill, we more than made up for with sheer will and determination. We had a great team spirit at Swansea, too, but that attitude isn't easy to find. Ainsworth told me there were no big-time charlies at Wycombe. Or, in other words, no egos. For them it was all about hard work, dedication and team ethic. That was all I needed to hear, and I didn't hesitate to sign.

As much as I try to unite the changing room for the good of the team, I think there have been several occasions over the years when players at certain clubs have resented me for whatever reason. I wouldn't say it's because they are jealous of my capabilities, but perhaps they are envious of my profile. Very often, my reputation precedes me. In the end, though, I do feel that I win over most players. As a striker, my job is to get goals, and there's no denying that a certain degree of selfishness comes with that. But as much as I play for myself, I'm always conscious of the team dynamic and how I fit into that. I often get players telling me that I'm a better player than they thought I was. I might come across as one-dimensional, or I might have played against them once or twice before and not done anything special, but when they start training and playing with me week-in, week-out, they see a whole different side of me. Saying that, I'm aware of the fact that ultimately, if someone did have a problem with me, they probably wouldn't come out and say so. There might be a lot of passive-aggressive stuff going on that I just don't realise. But they would have to come at me passive-aggressively because if they did it flat-out aggressively, we'd have to settle our differences like men and nine times out of ten they'd be going to sleep!

I rarely get my back up with the press. I understand they're just doing their job, and for the most part they help me do mine. But after I signed for Wycombe, a reporter asked me whether or not I felt I was a publicity signing. I said, 'No, of course I don't. I just came from a team who got promoted, I scored in the deciding game, I was top scorer the season before, and I'd won a shelf full of awards in the past couple of years.

Stats are stats. You can't argue with them. So where does the publicity element come into it?' Part of me can understand why people might think that. Wycombe are probably the first club I've been at that endeavours to utilise my social media presence in the sense that they run competitions on my Twitter account, etc. But in my opinion, that's symptomatic of them being a progressive, forward-thinking club, who are eager to capitalise on the changing game. If they want to use my social media presence for the good of the club, why not? It's not all one-way. It's mutually beneficial. Across all platforms I have over two million followers. As a lower league club, you'd be stupid not to try to utilise that in some way. It creates a stir, attracts new supporters and brings in sponsors. The way I was introduced to the fans was pretty cool. The club had a kit launch just before the season started, so they had a venue and about 300 fans showed up to see the unveiling. A few of the team paraded around in the new kits, then at the end they said, 'We have one more kit to show you!' Then I came out and a big roar went up. It was a nice moment.

They say it's a London club, but until training started, I didn't really appreciate how far away Wycombe was from my house. On an average day I have to leave the house by 7 a.m., get to training by around 9.30, leave the club at 1 p.m., then arrive home again around 3.30 or later, depending on traffic. It's a much longer day than at AFC Wimbledon, where I didn't have to get up until 8 a.m. There, I was home by 1.45. Even after I get home at 3.30, because I have so much going on these days, I might have a personal appearance to do, or a meeting to attend, a charity event, or some other business, all while there are four kids running around the house screaming for their dad. It's hectic, but it's the life I chose and I wouldn't have it any other way. When the kids aren't around it's too quiet!

• • •

Things don't always go according to plan. In my first game for Wycombe in pre-season I was sent off after 32 minutes because one of the opposition players was trying to bully Dayle Southwell, one of our youngsters. He got done by a vicious tackle, and I just saw red. I went rushing over and shoved the guy who'd made the tackle. I didn't think I shoved him that hard, but he went flying through the air like Tom Daley. Luckily, it was a pre-season game against the French side Le Havre, so it didn't have much bearing on the season proper. What it did do, though, was let everyone on my team know that physically, I had their back. From that moment on, the entire team knew that I was there to fight for them. Not literally, but in a footballing sense. I was going to give my all. It's a two-way street, though. I knew there'd be situations when I'd need them to have my back, like in the 89th minute and I'm expected to make a thirty-metre dash. I'm going to need one of the younger guys to step up and make that run for me!

Like I said, at Wycombe we have a great sense of togetherness. It doesn't matter if you're twenty like our youngest player, or you're thirty-six like our oldest. We're all in the same fight, and we all want the same things. We're not the strongest squad in the division, so the onus is on us to work for each other in order to make sure we achieve what we want to achieve. You need a hierarchy at a club, but an age barrier is still a barrier so it's important that it's inclusive rather than exclusive. Younger players need to know they have to work their way up. There's no room for prima donnas. I always tell them that with age comes knowledge and experience, and that's how you improve and push on. I'm not at the top, because there are players at the club who are older than me and have been here longer. One way that manifests itself is in displaying good manners in social situations. If there's only one seat available at a dinner, then I'll stand and let the guy who's older than me sit down. That's something I've tried to implement at every club I've played for. Whoever's the oldest carries the most influence. It's different from being a captain. To be a club captain is a huge responsibility and calls for a whole different skill set. It doesn't matter how old you are. I've seen twenty-one-year-olds who make fantastic captains. Me? I'd make a lousy captain. My time-keeping has been shit my entire career, and if you're a captain, of course you have to lead by example and be on time. I'm no captain, but I'm a leader and I'm good in the changing room. I think that was one of the reasons Gareth Ainsworth was so keen to get me at Wycombe.

Wycombe have a very distinctive style of play. They press and press and press. It's all about pressure and intensity. If I'm honest, that isn't really my natural game. But I'd been sitting on the bench for the best part of eight months at AFC Wimbledon, and I just wanted to go out there on the pitch and give it some. We had an indifferent start to the season, winning just one of our first seven games, and found ourselves in the relegation zone. League Two is very unforgiving. If you go on a bad run, clubs will be lining up to put the boot in. I hadn't started that many games, so I went to see the gaffer about it. I've always thought that if you sign a player, you play them. Otherwise, why sign them? Ainsworth told me he'd brought me in for my hold-up play, my eye for a goal, and my leadership qualities. I said, 'That's all well and good, but there must have been some miscommunication before I signed because here I am sitting on the bench. If I wanted to do that, I'd have stayed at AFC Wimbledon.' The chairman was involved in this discussion, too, and he said he questioned whether I was too big for the club. He said I regulated everybody else, so who regulated me? I told him my manager does. No matter how big my profile gets, what my personality is like, and what happens off the pitch, I'm still only one player in a squad.

I eventually managed to force my way into the team, and from mid-November we gelled and our form improved dramatically. We reeled off six wins on the bounce, and lost only once in thirteen games in the league. Things were going well, but in the midst of it all, something happened that took me right back to my days in Lithuania. On 19 November we played an away game at Cambridge United. Paul Hayes (Scunthorpe United, Barnsley, Preston North End) gave us an early lead from the penalty spot after which we pretty much controlled the game until the latter stages. Several times, I heard some racist comments coming from the stands. It was noticeable because you just don't hear it much these days. At least this time it was from an opposition fan, and not my own. Cambridge equalised late on, and then we grabbed a stoppage-time winner so justice was done in the end. On the field, anyway. I told the referee Trevor Kettle about the incident so he could put it in his match report, and after the game I sent out a tweet saying, 'Good 3pts 2day, great support again. It's a shame that a small group of Cambridge fans focus on colour rather than the game.'

Only a few years ago, I would have had to report it to the referee, then hope for the best. But having the kind of platform that I do means I can use it to not only make my feelings known but also raise awareness of various social issues, racism obviously being one very close to my heart. It had the desired effect. The tweet was retweeted hundreds of times, and a lot of genuine Cambridge supporters got in touch to say how disgusted they were at the behaviour of one of their own. In the days that followed, there was a big media furore and both the club and the police investigated the incident leading to at least one fan being banned indefinitely. People need to wake up and realise that while it has never been okay to say that kind of thing, maybe at one time they could get away with it. Now, they can't.

Our good league form coincided with our FA Cup run, where we beat Portsmouth, Chesterfield and Stourbridge, with me scoring in two of those games. I've always maintained that football, like life, should be fun and enjoyable, and when you score a goal it should be entertaining and funny. Life in itself is stressful, so any time you can diffuse that stress in any way, you should. That's why wherever I go, I do mad goal celebrations. The celebrations are important to me. It goes right back to when I did the bunny hop in Lithuania. At Doncaster there was the heel-and-toe dance, and at Northampton we had The Crane. After we scored, the whole team would lift their hand like a crane. Everyone wanted to know what it meant, so I said I would reveal all as soon as I bagged eighteen goals. The truth was, there was no story and I was trying to buy myself some time to think of one. It was all academic because I never reached the eighteen goals anyway. At AFC Wimbledon, I did a vote on YouTube and asked the fans to choose a goal celebration for me. They chose one called The Whip, but I only scored eight times that season so I decided not to tempt fate and never put it to a vote again. At Wycombe we do the *Toy Story* celebration where someone shouts, 'Andy's coming!' and we all fall to the ground at the same time. It's a re-enactment of the scene in the film when all the toys play around when nobody is there to see them, then play dead when Andy goes back to his bedroom. What I love about it is that it's not just the goalscorer and maybe the two nearest players doing it, it's pretty much the whole team. It brings us together and shows that we all belong to something bigger than just a football club.

Our FA Cup run culminated in a fourth-round glamour clash with Spurs. I was on the train when the draw was made, and my phone just went mad. Not only was it a London derby, but it was only about the second time Wycombe had ever reached that stage of the FA Cup. Spurs were flying at the time. There were over 31,000 at White Hart Lane for the match, and anyone who was there, or saw it on TV, will tell you that for the whole of the first half, despite being the Premier League team, Spurs couldn't touch us. We were 2-0 up! Nobody had bossed Spurs like that all season, especially on their own patch. I was up against Kevin Wimmer (LASK Linz, 1. FC Köln and Austria), the centre-back who'd been earning rave reviews only a week or two earlier for marking Sergio Agüero out of the game. I bullied him out of it and made him look ordinary. The quality of their bench proved the difference, as in the second half they were able to bring on Dele Alli and Mousa Dembélé and ended up winning 4-3.

Our league form suffered a bit in the aftermath, and it wasn't helped by the fixture congestion. We played six games in seventeen days in the second half of February, and didn't win any of them. Racism reared its ugly head again after the EFL Trophy semi-final against Coventry City. I went on at half-time and scored in a 2-1 defeat. After the game, someone who claimed to be a Coventry fan tweeted, 'Fuck off Akinfenwa you black prick.' I mean, you can call me a prick if you want, but leave the skin colour out of it. On that occasion, Wycombe had my back and the club reported the tweet. There's no place in the modern game for that kind of abuse. It's all a bit old. But, thankfully, incidents are getting increasingly rare. But nevertheless it was unfortunate that I was on the receiving end twice within a couple of months.

Every club has rules and a code of conduct, and Wycombe is no different. One of the rules here is that if you come in late, you are benched and don't play. No exceptions. The gaffer says he was never late for a game, and is proud of that fact to the point that he now holds everyone else accountable to his high standards. My time-keeping has always been a problem, and it's fair to say it has cost me a few starts at Wycombe. Moving towards the back end of the season, I was top goalscorer. The team was on a good run, and we had settled into a rhythm. At the beginning of April, I came in late for the Cheltenham game with Myles Weston and the gaffer dropped both of us to the bench. I know rules are rules, and I respect the gaffer for enforcing them, but this was a time I couldn't get behind the rule. In my opinion, a fine would hurt a player more and keep the strongest team available, which would be in everyone's best interests. The Cheltenham game was a big one, and we were going for a play-off place. We needed our strongest team out there. The match finished 3-3, which we were all pretty disappointed with. I'm not saying it would have been a different result had Myles and I played. The boys who did play did well. But it *might* have been different. We'll never know. Those two dropped points would prove crucial at the end of the season. The situation was made even worse when the club told me to accept liability and put out a tweet apologising for letting the team down. I wasn't going to do that. Not because I didn't respect the fans, but because I didn't feel wholly responsible. If the gaffer had given Myles and me a bit of leeway, it might never have got to that point.

It all came down to the very last game. We beat Cambridge at home with a goal from my young strike partner Scott Kashket (Leyton Orient, Welling United) after I headed the ball across the box, but other results went against us and forced us down into ninth place, just a point outside the play-offs. After what had happened the previous season at AFC Wimbledon, there wasn't a doubt in my mind that had we qualified for the play-offs we'd have gone on and won the final. I was just in that mindset.

At the end of the day, at Wycombe I silenced my critics once more by scoring eighteen goals in all competitions, and ending the season the club's top scorer. I played a lot of games, and was very happy with my contribution. At the end-of-season dinner, I went up on stage to receive the Supporters' Player of the Season, thanked everybody, and sat back down. Then a few minutes later, I was called up again to receive the Players' Player award. That was something I couldn't accept without calling the entire squad on the stage with me. It was a nod to the unity and togetherness we had as a squad and where that could take us. It was a very touching moment.

I was happy to sign with Wycombe for another season. But there's so much emphasis on me, and the formation we are playing, that I usually have to get the better of two centre-halves by myself for the team to work as a unit. I will take that responsibility on these big, broad shoulders, but it means I have to be an eight or a nine out of ten every game. Maybe my standards are just too high, but in my mind, I'm not playing at quite that level consistently enough. That's why now I feel another striker needs to come in. I play ninety minutes almost every game now, Saturday and Tuesday, which is a lot for a player whose body has been through what mine has. It's arrogant to think you can play well in every single game, especially when you're tired or carrying a knock. You have to always do what's best for the team, remember the club is bigger than you, and not be afraid to take a step back when it's required.

I thought that at my age the desire to play might start waning a bit. But as soon as pre-season started I realised that wasn't the case at all. I'm still as eager to play as I ever was. You miss playing in the summer. Not just the playing, but you also miss the structure and the camaraderie that football brings. I still feel like I have a lot to give on the pitch. We have a young, talented squad, and we're looking to make a big noise this season and beyond. There's no question this club belongs in a higher division than League Two and for me personally, I certainly don't feel like this is my last season in football. People have asked me if I'll be willing to drop out of the Football League in order to extend my career, and the answer to that question is yes. Probably. But it would have to be with the right club. As you get older you stop chasing the money and glory so much, and start looking for clubs where it just feels right.

11 #BEASTMODEON

A journeyman is a tag often levelled at me. I haven't stayed at a club longer than two-and-a-half years in any stint, and often it's a lot less. I've been on the books of fourteen different professional clubs, if you include Watford, where I was on youth terms. It was never the plan for things to work out that way. It was just the way it went. Like any business, football is unpredictable, and you just don't know where you'll be from one month to the next. But I do look back and think sometimes I was my own worst enemy. The reason I moved on so many times was that I knew that each time I went to a new club I would have to prove myself all over again. I needed that. I'm the type of player who could get too comfortable at a club, and that can easily turn into complacency. Having something to prove to yourself, or your employers, is the main thing, the main motivation, and everything else falls behind. First it's about proving you can do it, then when you reach a certain point in your career it becomes more about proving you can *still* do it.

Being a target man also means you have a very specific, some would say limited, range of skills. There will always be a requirement for big, strong players like me. But things change, and clubs change. What a club needs this season might be totally different to what they might need next season. A few times in my career I've been a victim of that. Perceptions change, or new managers come into a club and decide they want to try going down a different route and implement a different style of play that perhaps doesn't suit me.

My football, and how well I play, has often reflected my state of mind off the pitch. This ties in closely with my surroundings and my general happiness. I know that if I'm enjoying life, the football aspect will just fall into place. If I'm enjoying my time, I'll be enjoying my football, and as a striker that makes you more productive in terms of goals scored. Looking back, the times when I've haven't been scoring have been the times when I've been struggling off the pitch for whatever reason, or there's been some distraction or disruption around me. That's the key to consistency. Most of us can turn it on in fits and starts. Some of us can even turn it on on demand. But very few can turn it on week after week for any prolonged period of time.

I've always said I'm at my best if the club just lets me be me, and take care of myself. Every fitness coach I've ever worked with has taken one look and tried to impose his regime on me. He'll tell me to do sprints here, stretches there. I'm not saying any one way of working is any better than another. But the thing is, every system is different and they all think theirs is the best. Nobody knows me and my body, or the way I work, like I do. Of course this raises all kinds of issues with clubs and does cause a bit of friction. If a fitness coach is seen to let me get away with doing things my way, then he's going to have a bunch of players all refusing to do certain things because they don't fancy it. The difference is, no coach can ever say I don't do my bit, because I do. I'm not trying to get away with not doing things, it's just I have a different way of working.

I've always said I wouldn't want to be a manager, but it's something I'd like to try for three or four months just to see what it's like. I don't think I'd be able to be player/manager. That would be too much. But I want to see the football world from another perspective, do a job and then be able to step away with my head held high. Tactically, I wouldn't have a fucking clue. I'd need someone else to come and do that bit. But when it comes to getting the best out of my squad, I believe I'd be able to without a shadow of a doubt. When the chips are down, and we're dealing with adversity, I think I'd be able to make my players rise to the occasion and get results. That's where I would excel. The bottom line is I'd love to test myself in that arena, but I'd need a really good, experienced right-hand man.

Something I've always been interested in is the transition between player and manager, so when I met Jimmy Floyd Hasselbaink a while back at a Sky Sports event, I asked him about it. He said the main thing is that when you're a player, you can just look after yourself. But as a manager you have to look after the interests of twenty other players as well. It's not about you any more. There's the bigger picture. Because he was known in his playing days as being very opinionated, I asked him how he would manage himself, and he replied the only way to manage a player like himself is to be tough and lay down the law. Then I asked him how he would manage me, and he said the best way to manage a player like me is to let me go out there and be myself. Bully those I need to bully and get my goals. If I don't get goals, that's when I have to look at changing aspects of my game, or listening to other people who might have a different perspective on things.

In my mind, there's never a danger that my profile will outgrow whatever club I'm playing for. No matter what extra-curricular activities I get up to, I know that I'm still primarily a footballer. That's my job. That said, having a big profile in itself brings all kinds of opportunities that I never thought possible when I was growing up. I ended up doing a regular segment on *Soccer AM* with Razor Ruddock (Southampton, Tottenham, Liverpool, West Ham United and England), who was one of my idols. I can't believe I actually move in the same circles as celebrities of that calibre and stature. I was asked to do a BT Sport show recently with the boxer David Haye and Tim Westwood the DJ. That was unreal. David Haye knew all about me, but football not really being Westwood's thing, he didn't have a clue who I was. But we hit it off, and that night he gave me a shout-out on his radio show. I'm getting used to the attention now, but it's still very humbling.

I've done a lot of work for game developers EA Sports on the *FIFA* franchise since the whole 'Strongest Footballer' thing broke with KSI. When *FIFA 15* came out, to help promote it they asked me to sit on a panel with Joey Barton (Manchester City, Newcastle United, QPR and England), Kyle Walker (Tottenham, Manchester City and England) and Rio Ferdinand (West Ham United, Leeds United, Manchester United and England) and pick our ultimate team of the year. Just being there was an experience, because I was sitting at a table with three legends of the sport. Being in their company, and having the opportunity to put my opinions across and be treated as an equal by them, was very flattering. I didn't make the Ultimate XI, but I was cool with that because none of us did. It's quite hard when you're up against Ronaldo and Bale! For *FIFA 16* they did a survey and asked which players people were more excited to use in the game. Lionel Messi had 22 per cent of votes, and I had 78 per cent. That blew my mind. Last year, EA Sports set up an event called 'Finish the Fight' to launch the *UFC 2* video game where they matched me, boxer George Groves, ex-England rugby player Nick Easter and UFC fighters Luke Rockhold and Antônio 'Big Nog' Nogueira against each other to see who had the hardest punch. Luke Rockhold won. But, in my defence, he punches people in the face for a living, and I could probably do more keepy-ups than him.

I take being a father very seriously. It's a big responsibility. But maybe the things I take seriously, many other people wouldn't because I'm basically a big kid myself. I take on my kids in dance battles. To them, I'm an embarrassment but I am what I am. The fact that I have two daughters is one of the things that makes me want to keep lifting weights!

Eight years down the line, Ajani's mum and I still don't get on. But all I care about is doing right by my son.

Things have changed so much for me, especially in the past

few years. I go to award ceremonies now, and I look around and the place is full of A-listers. It's hard to accept the fact that this baller from a council estate in north London might be one of them. When I was growing up it would have been so easy for me to go down the wrong path. I don't think I ever would have instigated anything. I'm just not built that way. But I've always been big, and because of my size people into all kinds of mischief wanted me around for protection. Most of them knew how much I loved football, though, so they didn't try too hard to tempt me. Refusal often offends, as they say. Football and family kept me on the straight and narrow. I've been on quite a journey to get this far, and it's not over yet.

Whenever I go to an event, I don't go there to play a role, I go there to be me. But it just seems I get recognised a lot and people gravitate toward me, both celebrities and the public. When George Groves fought Carl Froch the second time for the WBA and IBF super-middleweight titles in 2014, I was part of the promo. With Groves being a London boy, I was more than happy to be involved when someone asked me. You have to rep your set. He did a bus tour from Stamford Bridge, him being a Chelsea fan, to Wembley Stadium, where the fight was being staged. Tamer Hassan the actor was there, Johnny Nelson the ex-boxer, a few other celebrities with London connections. I was there with my brothers, and the people who didn't know me automatically assumed I was a boxer. They couldn't believe it when I told them I played football for a living. The George Groves I met that day was nothing like the flash, arrogant Groves you see on the TV. That's just his fight persona, and I guess you need that. Those guys are gladiators, and you can't show any weakness or your opponent will be all over it. You also need to play it up for the cameras to generate interest. But I didn't know that before I met him. I was thinking I was going to have to match this flash, mouthy character. But the real George Groves is chilled and very respectful.

Groves put on a good show, but ended up being stopped in the eighth round. The fight turned out to be the biggest post-war boxing match the country has seen. Eighty thousand were there on the night, and it grossed about £22 million. For the bus promo we did we didn't quite get those kinds of numbers but it was a big part of the build-up and ended up on the news. Afterwards, people started saying to me, 'Wow, B, you are everywhere!' I was just honoured to be a small part of one of the biggest boxing events of the century. I've met Groves at a few events since, and we always have a chat.

Being a Liverpool supporter, the most astonishing experience of all was going for a burger with Stevie Gerrard. People say never meet your idols, but for me it's the total opposite. After I played against him for AFC Wimbledon, we stayed in touch.

He'd moved to LA Galaxy then, and told me that if I was ever in LA, to give him a shout. It so happened that a while later I was in LA with my brothers for the Black Entertainment Television (BET) sports awards. It was pretty plush and we had a good time.

After we arrived in LA, Stevie G promised to take us out to this cool joint at the Roosevelt Hotel called 25 Degrees, for what he described as 'the best burger in the world'. He told us to order what we wanted as it was on him, which is something you don't really want to say to group of big hungry black guys who just got off a plane. He wasn't joking about it being the best burger in the world. We stayed for about an hour chatting about his move. It all happened because when New York City FC signed Frank Lampard (West Ham United, Chelsea and England), LA Galaxy had to respond in kind. He also told me he thought I needed to take the Beast Mode brand to LA, because they're crazy about fitness there. It was a good talk. Weirdest of all, we were there sitting in this restaurant with Stevie G and not one person came up and asked either of us for a picture. The only people taking pictures was us! They soon got picked up by the British tabloids and before I knew it they were everywhere.

Earlier this year, I was out in LA again with my brothers and a few of my boys at a club in West Hollywood called Bootsy

Bellows. We booked a table, and it came with drinks. But me and my brothers were driving so we didn't want to drink. We were buzzing anyway. We saw a group of girls about to spend a ton of money on drinks, so we told them they could just come and sit at our table and drink ours instead if they wanted to. At the time, we didn't realise it was Malika and Khadijah Haqq, the Kardashians' best mates. So they came and sat with us and they were cool, down-to-earth girls. They asked me who I played for and I told them it wasn't one of the elite teams so they probably hadn't heard of us, but I had a big profile on social media and what have you. The next day they came to a gun range with us and shot some guns.

The twins wanted to plan every move with strategic accuracy, but I don't usually operate like that. I'm not that organised. If we're hungry, my friends and I will stop at a restaurant and eat. We don't often call ahead and make reservations and shit. But then I realised that was just what she was used to. If you're hanging with the Kardashians, one of the most famous families in the world, you can't just roll up to places. They need fair warning. We went out to STK's to eat, and the guy came over to read out the specials. The girls could tell that I was so lost in what he was saying. They had something basting, something else glazed. Something seasoned, something that's been marinating for three fucking weeks. The girls had to break it all down and explain it to me. I was just saying, 'Look, do you have wings or what?'

They ordered oysters and asked me if I wanted one. I said, 'What? Hell no. You'd better keep your oysters over there. I'm just here for the meat!' I ended up with ribs. Better than fucking oysters.

That same week, I was in a club out in LA and this guy grabbed me. I was instantly on the defensive. You never know who you're going to come up against. But it turned out to be Alex Oxlade-Chamberlain (Southampton, Arsenal, Liverpool and England). I told him the last time I saw him he was lifting the FA Cup. I'd been asked by FATV to go on the pitch and interview some of the players. One thing people can't fail to notice about me is that I'm really bad with names so I 'bruv' a lot of people off. Instead of using their name, I'll be like, 'What's up, bruv?' That day I grabbed Theo Walcott (Southampton, Arsenal and England) for an interview and clean forgot his name. I had to ask Alex Iwobi (Arsenal and Nigeria) who I know a bit, and the first thing he did was he ask me if I was drunk!

While I was interviewing Iwobi, he tapped Danny Welbeck (Manchester United, Arsenal and England) on the shoulder and got him involved. I'm sure at first he didn't know who I was. Not that he should. But I probably came across like just another person waving a microphone in his face. After that, I planned a trip to Toronto and Welbeck happened to be there. We hung out four days out of five. It was around the time that girl asked him for a picture then called him a dickhead. The pic went viral and then people started asking whether she'd called him a dickhead before or after she asked him for his picture. I was there when she took it. It was a ridiculous situation. He said he woke up the next day and his phone and email was just backed up with messages about it.

So I bumped into Alex Oxlade-Chamberlain in this club in LA, and Dele Alli happened to be in the same place at the same time. I'd played against Alli when he was at MK Dons and I was at AFC Wimbledon, so whenever we bump into each other we have a chat about the time I wanted to snap him in half. My friends are now seeing me hanging out with all these elite footballers, and people like the Haqq twins, and I remember one of them telling me I was moving in circles way above my station, but I looked like I belonged in that world. They kind of expect it with footballers, because we are in the same business and there's a kind of mutual respect. To me they're just normal guys who happen to play football. It doesn't matter if they're on TV or which club they play for. They're no better or worse than anybody else. But now they were starting to notice that bona fide A-listers were gravitating towards me, too. I have friends not just from all levels of football but from all across the sporting spectrum. I know some NFL and NBA players, some rugby boys. I love meeting people from all walks of life, and finding my place with them. I've developed a soft spot for American mainstream sports because they're so entertaining. *Any Given Sunday* and *Remember the Titans* are two of my favourite films.

The team I have around me is very small. I haven't even changed my agent in over a decade, because Dean knows me, and he knows what I want. By the time he brings a deal to me, I already know it's been vetted and it's the best possible deal out there for me. My younger brother, who is like my PA these days, always says he can't believe how far I've come in the past three or four years. It puts him in a position where he can sit down with people who want to form business relationships with me, reel off some stats, show them some footage and tell them what I can bring. I can see his point, but the thing is, I feel I haven't even started yet.

What does the future hold? Who knows? I'll be thirty-six this season, so I think it's fair to say I'm approaching the end of my playing career. This 2017–18 season might be my last, it might not be. I'll see how it goes, then next summer I'll reassess things. I have enough going on away from the playing side to keep me busy. I hope to start a football academy in south London in the near future, and use my profile to make it successful. The plan from there is to also have academies in north, east and west London, to offer the best possible framework, and after that we'll take it abroad. The main idea is to have a mentoring system, where young people are given guidance and support in the shape of a role model. I'll try to take it into schools and youth clubs, drawing on the experience I gained in youth work back at St Mary's, and it won't be limited to just young footballers. Other people need those things too.

With the BMO stuff, I just love the fact that I started it from scratch and it took off. It shows that anyone can do it. You don't need permission from anybody, or any special training. Just go and do it. It's been hugely successful here in the UK, so it might soon be time to expand and take it abroad. It's still early days for us, and we're still not sure where it will go. I don't really see myself as a fashion designer, so as long as the business is self-sustaining, that's enough for me. Pretty soon we'll be going large with BMO and shifting the focus away from clothing and onto games and fitness apps. People are always asking me questions about fitness and exercise, and I have a lot of information to put out there. I'm just excited to watch the brand evolve and see what it becomes, knowing that I created it from nothing. I'd like to do more presenting and other media stuff in the future. I flourish in situations where I'm allowed to just be me, and in fairness most of the outlets I work for recognise that and give me a free rein.

What I've learned is that you have to stand your ground. There have been times when they'll come to me and say they want to put me in a banana suit or have me running around with a tray of doughnuts or some shit and I'll be like, 'Fuck no. Are you mad?' Don't get it twisted, I don't mind having a laugh, but it's different when you're the one being laughed at. I'm very comfortable saying no. Someone told me once that if it doesn't feel right don't do it, no matter how much money they're offering. That has stuck with me. There's not enough money in the world to make me compromise my morality. Now when *Soccer AM* did the Chicken Wing Challenge I was all over that, because of how much I love chicken. I'm also due to sit down with the bigwigs at WWE within the next few months so there might be possibilities there. Never say never.

As for unfulfilled ambitions, I want to be in a Marvel film. I don't want to be an actor per se. I just want to be in a Marvel film. And *Game of Thrones*. I've already made the first move and put out some feelers through Vinnie Jones's agent, but if anyone reading this might be able to make it happen quicker, hit me up! I don't ever want to disregard any possibility. I don't impose restrictions on myself. The future is a big open space, where anything can happen. I know I'll do it well, because I will put my heart and soul into it. I want to evolve and grow as a person, and just see what opportunities arise. I like having my fingers in lots of pies, because life is like that. It's nice to be able to express myself, and not be put in a box. You either win or you learn that L is never a loss.

I'm optimistic that within the next ten years I'll have ticked all these boxes. Then I'll have a think about the next set of goals, and keep on moving forward. It's exciting. There are no limits. Nigeria is my spiritual home, but London is my real home and I love living there. For a lot of people, when they get older it gets too much for them and they don't want all the hustle and bustle. But I want the 'too much'. My life is all about hustle and bustle. Of course I want a bigger house and nicer garden, but I also want the Tesco Metro that's open until eleven, and the Nando's ten minutes' drive away. That's all I've known.

Whatever happens, I'm proud of what I've accomplished. I'm living proof that no matter what people say or think about you, if you work hard, persevere and have faith in your ability, you can achieve whatever you want. The mind is the most powerful thing you have. If you believe in yourself and stay focused and healthy, you'll put yourself on the right path. I love challenges, they keep you young. I don't just take them when they come, I actively seek them out. I'm always looking to test myself. That, to me, is the best way to grow as a person. That's one reason why I've changed clubs so often.

It's humbling to be a League Two footballer and have the profile I have. It shows that your mind is the most powerful weapon you have. Love me or hate me, you have to recognise that if you do anything for as long as I have been playing football you will evolve out of the box they try to put you in. It doesn't matter who you are or what you do, if people want to slag you off and find negatives, they will. That's the way it is. But once you come to terms with that, you'll be able to deal with it. People might look at me and point out that the highest level I ever played was League One. And they would be absolutely spot on. But there are thousands and thousands of players who didn't make it that far. Those same people might say my size is the reason I never got to the top, but that's something we'll never know. What I do know is that everything I did, I did my way. I've lived all my dreams, and I still am living them.

MY OFFICIAL FIRST XI

The club closest to my heart is Northampton Town, closely followed by Swansea City. But Portsmouth are probably my favourite fans to play in front of. They give me banter, like the 'Your tits are offside' thing, but at the same time they show appreciation. They give me stick, because they know I'm always going to give their team problems. There aren't really any sets of fans who I dislike, though Accrington Stanley supporters probably dislike me because of all the goals I've scored against them down the years.

People often ask me who would be in my First XI. In other words, who are the best players I've ever played with? I've thought about this a lot, and no matter who I pick I know I'm going to offend a lot of good people but this is it. I'd play a 3-4-3 diamond formation.

Goalkeeper: Mark Bunn

Centre-backs: Gary Monk in the middle, with Barry Fuller on the left and Kyle Walker on the right

Midfield: Roberto Martínez at the base of the diamond, with Leon Britton on the right, Andy Robinson on the left, and Giles Coke at the tip

Forwards: Lee Trundle would be the main man through the middle, on the right would be Cody McDonald, and on the left either Leon Knight or Saido Berahino, who are probably the best pair of finishers I have ever seen

The team might be a bit top-heavy with Swansea players but they'd make a good solid base and like I said, that was where I received my football education. I'd make space for Alex Russell from Torquay if I could, because he was also a baller and would slot right into that midfield. Maybe he'd be satisfied with a place on the bench next to Curtis Weston and Myles Weston from Gillingham. As defensive cover I'd have their old teammate Adam

Barrett, and Andy Barcham would round things out nicely. If I could have an entire squad, I'd have Sam Ricketts and Kevin Austin, and let's not forget Willy Guéret as a second goalkeeping option.

If I put myself in the team, my preference would be to form a strike partnership with Lee Trundle and still find room for Cody McDonald and either Berahino or Knighty. Okay, maybe I need to think about squeezing some defenders in somewhere. But that team would score a lot of goals!

ACKNOWLEDGEMENTS

I believe everyone has a story to tell: a beginning, a middle and an end. I find it rather mind blowing that here I am introducing you to mine for the world to read. Believe me, this book may be the start and the middle of my story but it is by no means the end. That may be yet to come!

I want to thank Damien McSorley for all his hard work and patience in collaborating with me to produce my story. Together we put in the long hours and forged a very close friendship. Thanks for all your help, bro.

It goes without saying I couldn't have achieved any of this without the support of my family. I'm all about family and your love and loyalty have made me the person I am today. Blessings as always. As well as being my family, my brothers are my best friends so Dele and Yemi, I want to thank you for always being there for me, my left and my right hand men.

To Dean Baker, my agent of 12 years. I trust you wholeheartedly with my football career. You are more than a friend. We are family. So much so that I will allow only you to represent the next generation of Akinfenwas – taking them to greatness!

My thanks to Claire-Louise Hinde and Duncan Ross at Wasserman. There have been many times you've gone above and beyond for me and I appreciate that.

Also, thanks to Richard Roper and the team at Headline. I bet we gave you some sleepless nights along the way but we got there in the end.

This isn't the Oscars, but I could be here thanking people all day because the fact of the matter is I had a lot of help on my journey. Football can be fickle, players and managers come and go, but I have friends for life thanks to football, particularly Clarke Carlisle, Myles Weston, Giles Coke and Jo Kuffour. I know I've forgotten so many people, so sorry to anyone I've missed out. If we're tight then you know who you are anyway.

To my captains: Adam Barrett, Garry Monk, Kevin Austin, Roberto Martinez, Barry Fuller, Paul Robinson, Chris Doig and many more players. Also to my many managers: I have learned from every one I've played under, whether it's good, bad or indifferent. I want to say a special thanks to Kenny Jackett from whom I learned so much, and I don't even think you'll know what I mean but you really helped me out. Thanks to Neal Ardley, and my current gaffer, Gareth Ainsworth. I went through something at the end of the 2016/17 season and you were ready to drop everything and fly out to meet me to talk things through. I don't forget stuff like that.

Lastly I want to acknowledge all the people that doubted me, not because I proved you wrong but because I proved myself right.

PICTURE CREDITS

All images © Adebayo Akinfenwa, except the following:

P2: top right; top left; centre right; p.3 top two images © Kii Studios

P4: bottom left: © Matthew Ashton – AMA/ Getty Images

P4: bottom right © David Horn/PRIME Media Images Limited

P6: centre © Mike Hewitt/Getty Images; p.6 bottom: © Paul Gilham/Getty Images; p.7 top: © Adrian Dennis/AFP/Getty Images; p.7 bottom © Jordan Mansfield/Getty Images

P6: top © David Cornwell Photo Images

P8: top left © Andrew Matthews/PA Archive/PA Images